Stock Mark
Beginners
Learn Strategies To Profit In Stock Trading, Day Trading And Generate Passive Income

Table of Contents

Introduction

This guidebook is going to spend some time taking a look at the stock market and how you can get started. We will start out with some information on what the stock market is all about, some of the benefits of choosing this as your vehicle for investing, and even some of the different options that you can choose from when you are ready to invest in this market.

Many people have considered going into the stock market, but they are worried that they won't be able know how to enter the market or they will not find the right strategy that can help them be successful. This guidebook is going to help with this problem because it provides you with some of the best strategies possible, that even a beginner can get started with and see success in no time.

Have you ever heard of technical analysis, fundamental analysis, income investing, the CAN SLIM strategy, or anything else that is similar to this? These are all strategies that can be very useful when it comes to working in the stock market, and all of them can help you get a great return on investment when you get started.

In addition to talking about some of the great strategies that come with the stock market and all the different options that you can work with, you are sure to find a lot of great information, tricks, and tips that will ensure you can see success as a stock market investor. Even beginners can be successful in this endeavor, and this guidebook will give you the tools that you need to make sure that you attain the goal you want.

Whether you are a beginner or a beginner to investing in general, or you have been investing for some time, and you are now interested in starting out with the stock market for the first time, this guidebook will have all the strategies, tips, and tricks that you need.

Chapter 1: Stock Trading

Everything must start somewhere. That's true even for this book! So then the question is raised of "where should we start?" After all, stock trading is an immensely dense topic, and there's a huge number of different things that make it up.

My goal in this book is to make stock trading easy for you to understand. By the end of this book, I'm hoping that you're going to have a firm grasp on stock trading and important stock trading strategies.

But to get there, we're going to have to start from somewhere a little bit simpler! So let's start by discussing what stock trading is, and where modern stock trading comes from.

Stock trading is, in essence, the idea of trading shares of a corporation; however, when people say stock trading without a more exact definition, they're often including all branches of investing, such as options trading, bonds, and any other kinds of securities.

We'll get into all of those definitions later, but for right now, we just need to focus on the core concept. So what is a stock? Well, stocks can be defined as a share of a company. That is to say that when you own a stock, you are partly an owner of that company. There's a little bit more to this, though; for example, there are actually two separate stock markets that stocks can be bought and sold on, and the most popular one is actually the market most distended from actual impact on a company.

So all of this said, how does one actually make money on the stock market? One always hear about people who have gained an absurd amount of money from investing, but nobody actually makes it clear how they do that.

Well, fortunately, you don't need a doctorate in economics or finance to make a fortune on the stock market. However, at the same time, you should certainly temper your expectations; if you're expecting to become a millionaire stock trader, then the reality is that this is most likely not going to happen. You could always be the exception, of course, but most people who invest in the stock market don't become millionaires; otherwise, everybody would be a millionaire!

On the other hand, though, what you can expect is that if you follow good practices, you can learn what you're doing sufficiently enough to make a pretty decent amount of money on the stock market. I'd go as far as to say that if you have a knack for it, you could even turn quite a pretty penny. I wouldn't promise you millionaire status, but if you're good at what you do, you'll probably reap some sort of reward.

So how does one actually make money on the stock market? Well, that depends upon the types of investments that you're making as well. If you're truly focused on stocks, then your money will be coming largely from a combination of the dividends paid by the stock as well as the cash value of the stock itself upon selling it. This, of course, isn't guaranteed; the dividends will generally reflect upon the profit of the company, and the cash value of the stock will do the same.

That said, this is why smart investing is so heavily rewarded on the stock market. With some clever investing and some financial common sense, you can make a good amount of money.

Trading stocks essentially come down to buying and selling these shares to companies. When a company is particularly profitable, it pays to have their stock so that you can receive their stock's dividend payments. This essentially means that people ultimately end up wanting to own these stocks, believe it or not. They always want them for the fact that when a company is profitable, their dividends increase, which in turn makes the stock more profitable and more valuable.

So in essence, if it's a simple question of what stock trading is, then the answer is equally simple: stock trading is simply the passing back and forth off pieces of companies. When you own a piece of a company, you're entitled to some part of the profit that the company makes - we'll discuss this a bit more in the next chapter.

In essence, one can consider a corporation to be a bit of a cooperative structure. That is, if you own a part of the company, you truly become in a sense a part owner of the company. In most cases, you're entitled to the right to help the company make decisions and to help steer the company. When you own a stock of a corporation, you are thereby generally allowed to have some sort of say in the decision-making process. At the very least, you can trust that the business will be acting with the stockholders' interest in mind because that's the corporation's primary responsibility.

All in all, stock trading isn't nearly as intimidating as people like to act like it is. A lot of people will tell you that you need a lot of special training or classes to start, but that's not true at all. In reality, all that you need is a little know-how, a little luck, and a lot of common sense. If you've got these things, then you should be on the path to becoming a pretty solid stock trader. Read on to learn about the different kinds of stocks and securities so that you can prepare yourself to become an expert stock trader.

Chapter 2: Basics of Fundamental Investing

Fundamental investing really boils down to investing in a company because you believe in what the company is doing and its potential. This requires a lot more work than technical trading.

With technical trading, your data points basically begin and end with the performance of the stock. Now, your data set can extend for a long time in the past and can be projected quite some time in the future, but it only comes from one place. It only comes from the actual performance of the stock. There is no other source of data points. This gives you a greater sense of control.

With fundamental investing, you're focused on three key questions. Is the company making money? Will it continue to make money in the future? How well does it compare to others in its industry?

Now, it may seem that these questions are pretty simple and straightforward, but it really boils down to how you get information to answer these questions. Many analysts could try to answer these questions regarding a particular company and come up with completely different answers.

Fundamental investing, ultimately, is all about the midterm to long term value of the company. It's not really the stock itself that you're paying attention to, but the company's quality, how well it's doing, and how likely it is that it would do better in the future.

Another key aspect of fundamental investing is that you are looking for bargains. That's the bottom line. Either you are looking for a company that is underpriced by the market now or in the future.

It's easy to understand the first scenario. For example: Company A is doing really well in its industry. It is a market leader, has great products in its development pipeline, and possesses a tremendous client base. Still, it's in an industry that is, for some reason or other, not very sexy. Similarly, its growth rate is not as stunning as internet companies or other technology-based companies.

While this company is making more money than companies in sexier industries, it doesn't matter to the market. The market thinks that this company is simply just not interesting enough. However, when you look at the cash flow of the company, how much debt it has, and all other important factors, you can see that there is a tremendous amount of discounting going on as far as its market valuation. There's a big disconnect between what its stock price should be based on its earnings and earnings potential and what the company currently trades at.

The analysis above estimates the hidden value of the company as it stands now. There is also another way to do fundamental investing: forecasting a company's future worth.

Warren Buffet and other legendary investors often work this way. They don't mind paying a premium for a company now because they are so confident that the company is going to perform even better in the future, that they're actually getting in at a discount. This is one aspect of fundamental investing that you should also pay attention to.

The Big Challenge in Fundamental Investing

Trying to find a discount now, as far as the actual value of the company as it exists now, is actually getting harder and harder. As more analysts and value investors flood the market, there is less and less of these 'undervalued' companies because the price per earnings ratio of these companies tends to get bid up.

Now, these fundamental stock plays are not going to be at the same level as growth stocks, but their prices do tend to get bid up. The better approach would be to disregard their high prices now because, based on your projections, you see this company being a bargain based on its future performance.

Fundamental Investing Goals

What are the goals of people who invest using a fundamental investing strategy? First of all, they buy stocks in companies with solid fundamentals that are either low priced now or can be justifiably bought now at a high price because of projected future growth.

It's still the same strategy. You're looking for some sort of "under appreciation." You're looking for some sort of discount. There has to be some sort of disconnect between what the company is truly worth and its price currently or its price in the future.

What are the Fundamentals of a Company?

The operative word in the phrase "fundamental investing," of course, is "fundamental." So what is so fundamental about "company fundamentals?"

First of all, you're going to use financial statements issued by the company. These are required by law from public companies. Officer of a public company are required to make public their financial statements.

As a fundamental investor, you're going to look through a company's quarterly and yearly filings. You would then get a clear idea of the company's quarterly and yearly revenue, its income, and its growth trend. You are also going to pay attention to its profit margin, as well as its debt load and return on equity.

What is Return on Equity?

Return on equity measures how much profit the company produces per dollar invested in the company. This highlights the fact that the company is able to turn whatever amount of money is invested in it and grow it by a certain rate. Now, the bigger the rate, the better.

How do we arrive at ROE or return on equity? Take the total amount of money invested in the company and divide it by the amount of profit generated by the company. This is your ROE.

It determines whether the company seems like it's making money but is actually burning through a lot of cash just to produce income, or it's an actual money generator. Because you know you are looking at a very attractive company when it takes a fairly low amount of cash and is able to multiply it. The more cash it generates from actual investment inputs, the better that company looks.

Pay Attention to the Company's Overall Ability to Produce
Positive Cash Flow

Cash flow is one of the most important factors a fundamental
investor looks at. In fact, Warren Buffet makes a big deal out of cash
flow. If you determine that a company has a positive cash flow pretty
much throughout the year, then you can be more confident in the
company. You would know that this company does not suffer from
structural or operational weaknesses that may put it at a serious
disadvantage if certain conditions come to pass.

For example, if a company suffers certain cash flow bottlenecks
consistently throughout the year, this may be due to the fact that most
of its money is tied up in accounts receivables. As long as that money
can be successfully billed from the companies and individuals who owe
that money, then the company is going to be making money.

What if for some reason or other the company's industry suffers a
downturn and institutional clients can't produce the cash? This is going
to be a serious issue.

The good news is you can see this a mile away when you look at the
cash flow figures of a company. You can see whether it has a wide base
of customers. You can see whether it has a diverse range of customers
across a few industries. You can also see whether there are structural
limits to where its cash is coming from.

Make Earnings Estimates for the Future

Another aspect of fundamental investing is that you make earnings
estimates for the future. You don't just look at what the company is
doing right now. For all intents and purposes, chances are, the
company's performance right now is already baked into its stock price.
Instead, you're going to make an educated guess as to how well it would
do in the future. Based on current earnings, you're going to project its
earnings estimates into the future.

Of course, this is not as simple as it may seem. You can't just do
a straightforward projection. For example, if a company grew by 5%

in the past 10 quarters, it doesn't make sense for you to automatically assume that it's going to grow at that same rate. You have to factor in what's going on in the general economy, the health of the specific industry the company is in, the state of the competition, and the specific growth rate of the different parts of the company. In other words, the projection must be conditioned by other factors. Otherwise, you might just be fooling yourself into thinking that, since the company has grown steadily in the past, then this automatically means it will continue in the future.

Conditions do change. Often times, they change overnight. Don't automatically assume the same growth rate. Factor in realistic parameters.

Beware of Expert Earnings Estimates

If you think you might have a tough time making earnings estimates for a company you're thinking of investing in or a company that you have already invested in, wait until you look at the work of experts. There are many stock market experts and company analysts. In fact, there's too many of them.

The problem is, a lot of them are associated with or come from' prestigious' trading houses and investment banks that it's too easy to give too much weight to them. Many investors think that as long as the estimates are 'official' statements of well-respected investment banks, they should trust it automatically. You have to look through the numbers the 'experts' processed and see if you would come to the same conclusion.

The good news about these analyst reports is that they include all the numbers that they considered when coming to their conclusions. They open this information so anybody who has the time and attention to detail can check out those numbers for themselves. It is your job to see if the numbers reasonably support the conclusions of the analysts.

You have to do this yourself. At the very least, skim or scan through the materials. Don't just agree automatically.

Product Pipeline Considerations

Another key factor to consider when doing fundamental analysis is how broad the product pipeline of the company is. This is very important because there are many companies who are making a lot of money, but their product lines are mature. In other words, it's going to be a long time until a new crop of products replaces their top earners. This is a big issue for pharmaceutical companies and other industries where patents expire over time.

Pay attention to this issue because you might be stepping into a trap. You might be buying into a company that may be on its way to a long, painful decline. It may have started already. You think you're getting into this amazing multinational big brand pharmaceutical company, but it turns out that a lot of their blockbuster drugs are already turning generic or only have a few years left of patent protection.

Don't get caught by surprise. Make sure that the product pipeline of the company that you are thinking of buying is robust enough to sustain continued growth. In the case of pharmaceutical companies, be clear on their patent acquisition plans-if they can't come up with products on their own, they should have solid plans for buying smaller companies with promising patent applications or current products.

Balance Sheet Analysis

Balance sheet analysis really gets to the heart of the value of the company. Seriously. If there are any two pieces of official, legally mandated disclosures that you absolutely need to pay attention to as a fundamental investor, it's the balance sheet and cash flow analysis.

The balance sheet simply takes the company's liabilities and deducts it from the company's assets. What's left is shareholder equity or the net worth of the company. This gives you a big picture view of what this company is truly worth.

Management Analysis

Depending on how long you've been investing and how many manager profiles you've checked out, management analysis might be useful for you. Pay attention to how visionary the leadership is.

Please understand that in corporate America, corporate competence is assumed. In other words, a company's officers are presumed to already know how to do their jobs. The big issue is whether they have a good idea as to what to do. In other words, do they have vision? The bigger the company, the higher the chance that it's going to attract top notch operators. These are people who know how to do things.

The big question: are they being guided by top brass leadership to do the right things that would position the company for continued dominance in the future or position the company for even greater heights? How do you analyze this factor when selecting stocks?

First of all, pay attention to how visionary its leadership is. Look at their official 'vision' statements or other public 'vision' statements. Pay attention to the track record of the results the team produces. Take a look at whether the results tend to grow over time. Finally, pay attention to the CEO. How long has he or she been on the job?

If the CEO has been at the helm for a long time, then you should think about succession issues. Who is slated to replace the CEO? Again, apply the analysis above to the successors. How visionary are they? Do they have a track record of producing results?

Sales Analysis

It's also important to look at the overall sales of the company and see if it is growing on a quarter over quarter basis. Now, a few dips here and there are okay. However, the company should be growing and it should be growing at a robust pace. If not, chances are other companies would look more attractive by comparison.

Disclaimer: don't hang your hat on this. This is not the one answer that should make you buy a stock or skip it. However, it does lay the foundation as to whether the company has a future. If sales are growing at a healthy clip on a quarter by quarter basis, then, with everything else being equal, this is a company to pay attention to.

Operating Income vs. Actual Income

Another way fundamental investors dissect companies is to pay attention to their operating income and compare it to their actual income. Income analysis is extremely important. The good news is, by law, the securities and exchange commission in the United States, requires public companies to release income statements. This is called 10K and 10Q filings. Pay close attention to these documents.

These documents are presented in a fairly clear way. You just need to look at certain lines in the report. First of all, you need to look at the net income line. This will tell you the profit the company earned... This is net income.

Sounds pretty straightforward, right? Well, not quite. You have to pay attention to non-recurring income or extraordinary charges.

For example, it may seem that a company lost money for the quarter. It may even be a very big loss. But if the report states that it is a one-time charge because the company's laying off people or shutting down divisions, you need to look closer. Why? When you discount these extraordinary items, it may well turn out that the company is actually making money.

Similarly, if the company made a tremendous amount of money in the past quarter, take a look as to whether this is non-recurring income or an extraordinary windfall. Sometimes, companies get a huge infusion of cash because they sold off a division or they sold off some assets. This may seem exciting because the net income blew up, but when you discount those, it may well turn out that the company is bleeding money and not doing really well.

In order for you not to get thrown off by the net income line, you should focus instead on reading income statements with an eye towards operating income. This is actual income from normal operations.

By normal operations, we're not talking about selling a division of the company or selling assets or any one-time situation. We're also not talking about adjusting tax brackets, which can only be done infrequently. Instead, we're talking about normal income generating operations. This is how well the company usually does on a day to day basis.

One key shortcut to determining operating income is to pay attention to a reporting line that says "earnings before interest, taxes depreciation and amortization" or EBITDA. This should give you a clear idea of the operating income of the company you are analyzing.

Cash Flow Analysis

In addition to income analysis, cash flow analysis is one of the most important analyses you could do if you are pursuing a fundamental investing strategy. With cash flow analysis, you pay attention to net income versus cash flow.

Net income really boils down to total profit. Revenues minus costs. This is a problem because sometimes, it can hide expenses, depreciation or credit costs. Cash flow, on the other hand, makes it much harder to hide these things. It also makes it harder to hide structural weaknesses in the company.

With cash flow analysis, you get to measure temporary losses that fund all the operations. You get a clear idea of a company's obligations and debts as well as the promotions it does. This analysis gives you such a clear view of a company's prospects that you should look for companies that have enough cash to cover all debt. It should have enough resources to take care of all marketing and operations and have cash left over for additional future projects.

If you look at the cash flow statement of a company and it shows that the firm experiences negative cash flow (at least two times per year), this should be a red flag to you. This highlights the fact that the company might be suffering from structural issues. It still makes a profit overall, but this provides cold comfort because there are certain rough patches the company goes through every single year. If you don't see this and business conditions change, it doesn't take long for that negative cash flow to translate into a loss for the year.

Where does negative cash flow stem from? It can be due to a small customer base restricted to a narrow range of industries or is restricted to just one industry. It can also arise when only one customer accounts for almost all the sales of the company. Cash flow issues can reflect the fact that most of the products sold by the company are sold on credit. This is the accounts receivable scenario I described earlier. Finally, cash flow issues also tend to shed light on slow product development.

Be very suspicious and concerned if any of these are in play as revealed in the form of negative cash flow. This doesn't necessarily mean that you have to completely avoid the company or just give up on it. Instead, this should prompt you to dig deeper as to its fundamental value and see if there are any other points of attraction in the company.

Earnings Per Share Analysis

Take the total net income of the company and divide it by the total number of shares outstanding. This gives you an earnings per share figure. Now, the next step is to take the current price of the company's stock and divide it by the earnings per share. This gives you a price per earnings ratio.

Now, what do you do with this ratio? Well, it's all comparative. You look at other companies in the same industry as the company you're analyzing and make sure that they share the same fundamentals. You don't want to compare apples to oranges. You want to make sure that you're comparing pretty much similar companies who deal with the same fundamentals.

After you have lined up these companies, pay attention to their price/earnings ratio or P/E. This should highlight which companies are expensive, which companies are relative bargains, and what is the industry average P/E.

Once you have these figures, compare these numbers with the P/E of companies in the overall stock market. By doing all these comparisons, you should get a fairly clear idea as to whether a company is trading at a bargain or whether it's overbought or overvalued.

Cash Flow Per Share Analysis

Take total cash flow figures from the operations of the company and divide it by the shares outstanding. You then compare this figure with cash flow per share figures from other companies within the same industry. Again, this should give you a fairly clear picture of how that company stacks up to the competition in terms of investment potential.

Combine Cash Flow and P/E Analysis

The next step is to combine both the figures you get from your cash flow and P/E analysis to determine which stock is underpriced. Many stock experts say that cash flow analysis is the best way to value and compare stocks.

Once you reach this stage, you have all the data that you need to properly compare stocks. You can only tell if something is a bargain if you compare it to something else.

You have to line them up and see where the numbers fall. You can't just automatically assume that since the company reached a certain threshold that it is necessarily a good deal. Don't compare it with itself or compare it so some sort of abstract ideal. Compare it to other companies in its industry.

Look for strengths that a company has that others don't have. On the flip side, always look for weaknesses that it has that others don't have and cross reference these or support these with the financial numbers they are legally required to supply. Once you have everything together, you can then properly size up which companies are good deals and which ones are trading at a steep premium.

Chapter 3: How Does The Stock Market Work?

The mechanism by which the stock market operates is really no rocket science. The stock markets operate similarly to an auction house, where buyers place bids, and sellers try to reach a consensus. Stocks are commonly traded on exchanges, and a prominent example is the New York stock exchange.

As mentioned previously, companies that are interested in selling shares are listed on the stock exchange, for potential investors. Companies do this often in a bid to expand their businesses. The prices of shares fluctuate as the demands vary. For example, a company with recognized prospects of success would have investors swarming towards its stocks, causing an increase in price.

Companies aspire to be listed on the stock exchange as it guarantees visibility in the stock market and liquidity for their shares. There are criteria to be met before a company can be listed on the stock exchange.

These are provided by regulatory bodies such as the financial industry regulatory authority. Most of the requirements such as listing fees constricting and regulations, prove to be tough for newly founded cooperation.

Therefore, other methods of trading are employed. Listed companies that trade directly are involved in what is termed a 'primary market'.

A secondary market, on the other hand, involves investors buying stocks from other investors. The sellers purchase the stocks, and when there is an increase in stock price, sell it out to another investor.

A secondary stock market is slightly similar to an over the counter [OTC] stock exchange. OTC stocks are not listed on any formal stock exchange like the NYSE. Rather, they are listed on specialized over the counter bulletin boards [OTCBB], or pink sheets. They provide other options to companies that cannot afford to meet formal exchange lists criteria.

For example, Johnson buys a stock when it is $10. The next day, the price of the stock rises to $15, and he sells it to another investor, thus procuring a 50% profit. On the downside, the shares could drop to $5, and he would record a 50% loss. Secondary markets, OTC's, usually require an intermediary such as a broker, and their stocks are called unlisted stocks.

A stock market index, is a summary of a fraction of the stock market's performance, and it could either be market-cap-rated, or price rated. The Dow Jones Industrial Average [DJIA], is one of the most predominant stock market indexes in use, and it is price rated. Other examples are the Wilshire 5000 and the S&P 500. Indices basically serve as an evaluation of the risks, benefits, and earnings of companies on the market.

History of the Stock Market

It's a known fact that man is inherently selfish, in the broad sense of always wanting to gain from any venture. Imagine you have a billion-dollar idea to execute, but there was not enough capital. The government provides little help, and the wealthy in society demand incredulous interests for their loans. This was the dilemma faced by business owners in the past. But in the persistent nature of man, they developed a means to circumvent this situation. They began to technically sell bits and pieces of the company, so as to generate capital for a startup.

For instance, they would convince a person to buy 5% shares, with the promise of a 5% profit from the company in the future. In 1602, the Dutch East Indian company became the progenitors of this idea on the Amsterdam stock exchange.

Stock markets were established when countries in the new world commenced trading with each other. They organized what was known as a joint stock exchange, by pooling their savings together and owning shares in each other's businesses. The idea was incredibly successful, that it spread rapidly to other parts of the world. The Dutch, as previously mentioned, were the originators of this idea.

As the idea yielded prolific results, a need arose for a centralized environment to exchange shares. Therefore, London stock traders resolved to start meeting in a coffee house, and in 1773, they bought the coffee house. They renamed it the 'stock exchange.' The waves moved into America, and the Philadelphia stock exchange was the first to be set up in 1790.

The infamous New York Stock exchange [NYSE], was created in 1817. And it is currently one of the most powerful stock exchanges in the world based on market capitalization. Most people hear 'wall street' and immediately correlate it with the stock market. The stock exchange market on Wall Street opened on May 17, 1792, 24 brokers signed the Buttonwood agreement under a buttonwood tree.

By 1971, Nasdaq was founded and this posed a stiff competition to the NYSE. The Nasdaq used electronic evolution to its advantage, and investors found this favorable as securities were liquid. The NYSE responded to this by listing themselves and merging with Euronext in 2007. Thus, the first transatlantic stock exchange was created.

Over the years, the stock market has experienced significant setbacks, as expected of an authentic, highly competitive field. But the bounce backs have been rewarding and experiences learned, are used to prevent future occurrences.

Why You Should Invest In the Stock Market

There is a common misconception that investing in the stock market is synonymous with gambling. Although no magic formula has been created to guarantee success in the stock market, there are perks to it. The stock market is a great place to invest in, if you employ the right strategies, and overcome your fears. The stock market is not a black hole where life savings are aggressively sucked into, and here is why.

- Long term advantages; Warren Buffett advise that a stock shouldn't be touched when it is less than five years at least. Lock in periods do not apply to the stock market, this means that you can hold the stock for as long as you want. And the flexibility allows you to sell the stock whenever you want as well. It is for this attribute that stocks are advisable for people investing towards a long term goal such as retirement or education.

- Dividend income; stock returns are generally derived from capital gains and dividends. A capital gain is attained when you sell a stock at a higher price than you purchased it. While dividends are a part of the profit that a company gives its shareholders over a period of time, capital gains are more rewarding, but for those looking to minimize risks, dividends albeit little, are readily available.

- You can easily diversify; the stock market has earned a reputation for being volatile. Rather than piling up your spare cash in a dormant low-interest savings account, you can make it work for you. Alongside stocks, other securities can be purchased on the stock market, and in the event of one failing, another rises. Mixing up your stocks with bonds, CD's and other fixed income securities are generously rewarding in the long run.

- It doesn't require much to start with; compared to other forms of investment like real estate or gold, you do not need a lot of money to begin. The stock exchange lists thousands of companies. And there are stocks that are really cheap to purchase. This counters the idea of huge risks for huge rewards, but hunger for immediate profits is irrational in investments.

- Mergers pose a reward; when companies unify, or a company is bought by another, the stock price elevates considerably. By tactfully watching out for possible mergers, an investor is likely to benefit from such great opportunity.

- You solely take decisions; the stock market presents you with the chance to make independent decisions, regarding the type of investment you're interested in. You can also determine the extent you want to go. Playing it safe or going all out is totally up to you, as opposed to other forms of controlling investments.

• The process is visible; the stock market is well secured by the action of regulatory bodies. In the past, the absence of regulation led to losses as fake companies sprouted. But now, the highs and lows are for everything duly documented on the Internet. The ability to clearly see the mechanisms behind gains and losses is an added advantage.

• Stress-free trading process; the emergence of online trading platforms has resulted in the simplification of stock market trading. With just a click, stocks can be bought or sold. Also, since physical interactions between buyers and sellers are not necessary, commission paid to brokers isn't so much anymore.

• Liquidity; transactions in the stock market are a given, therefore it is relatively easy to get in and out of stocks.

• Stock ownership puts you ahead in a developing economy; an economic boost activates a series of events that the stock owner is not left out of. It increases cooperate earnings, and this, in turn, creates income and sale of goods. And this ultimately boosts a business' profit. And guess who rakes in a certain percentage of the company's profit?

Chapter 4: Options I Can Choose to Invest In with the Stock Market

You may be surprised to learn that there are actually a few different options that you can work with when it comes to investing in the stock market. When you enter the market, you will want to pick from a certain niche and work with a specific strategy in order to ensure that you get the results that you are looking for with the investment.

The choices that you make may depend on things like what is available, the amount of capital that you have to use in the first place, and how much risk you are comfortable when you start out. Even with a good amount of research and a good strategy in place, many investors need to remember to have some skepticism when starting to help them manage their risks and actually pick the right option that will bring them a profit.

In this chapter, we are going to explore the different options that you can choose when you get started with the stock market. These options all have some positives, and it often depends on which one works with the overall plan that you have.

Some of the different options that you can choose from when working in the stock market include:

Investing in Dividend Stocks

If you are using an investment strategy based on a long-term investment in a stock, then there are really quite a few stocks that you can choose for this strategy. Many companies offer stocks that pay dividends, which is where you can earn an income quarterly or yearly for as long as you hold onto the stock. As long as you make good selections in the stocks that you want to work with, you will actually make a great income from your choices and won't have to do as much with the stocks.

While there are plenty of choices to go with when you look for dividend stocks, you must remember that not all the stocks on the market are going to be dividend stocks. Make sure to do your research and ensure that you are finding the right ones to work with.

First, it is important to understand how a particular stock can yield a dividend to you, and then you can screen through a few companies in order to help you pick the right company to invest in. Your screening process needs to include a look at how the company makes a profit, how much of the profits they retain, and more. The good news is that all companies that are traded on the stock exchange will need to release financial statements. These documents can go a long way to helping you figure out which ones make a profit and are a good option to invest your money in.

Once you have gone through and come up with a good list of stocks that you know will pay you a dividend and that you are interested in, you then want to narrow down that list even more to help you check that you pick out high-quality stocks. Some of the things that you should consider looking at to help you figure out whether a particular dividend stock is the right one for you to invest in includes:

• The company has dividend payments that are uninterrupted. You should look back as far as you can to see if there is ever a time when the dividends are missing.

• Look out for how high the return on equity is. If you look at the average over five years, it should be around 15-20%.

• Look for rising earnings and rising sales for each share.

• Look for the growth in dividends. The best companies are going to have a growth of this dividend being at least 5 % over the past ten years.

Taking the time to look for these answers can make it easier to rank out all the companies that you are interested in investing int. Depending on the answers that you get, you should be able to pick out the right company to invest your money in.

Investing in Foreign Stocks

Some investors who have spent time in the market will decide to diversify their portfolio even more and will work in foreign stocks. This can also be a good place for a newer investor to get started in too, as long as you take your time to learn that market. There are a lot of foreign companies that are promising, and you may be able to get a great return on your investment if you are careful.

There is a good deal of risk that comes with these foreign companies, and this is something that you shouldn't ignore at all. You need to learn about foreign markets before entering and find out if there are different rules and regulations that could influence how well your investment goes. However, despite some of the risks, the foreign exchange market can be a great place to invest. Some of the benefits of going with this market include:

• Foreign stocks are going to represent an added opportunity for investing. You may find that it is hard to find the local company that you want to work with, but depending on what you are looking for, you may be able to find that company internationally.

• It helps with diversifying. You need to make sure that you are spreading out the risks that come with your investment. One way to do this is to use more than one company when you are investing. Adding in some foreign stocks can make this easier.

Of course, it is important to not overlook some of the risks that come with these foreign stocks. Some big risks come from these including from the exchange rate. Your return on the stock could end up catering for currency exchange rates from the currency of that country over to your own. The economy of another country, not the economy of yours, will determine how much you can earn or lose. You should probably be careful when it comes to investing in countries that are suffering from social and political issues.

However, even though there are some bigger risks, in the long run, it can also mean that you will have more rewards when you reach the end. If you can find a good company overseas to work with, you can make a big return on your investment.

Investing in Penny Stocks

Another option that you can choose to work with are penny stocks. These are a type of stock that often have a much smaller share price than traditional stocks, which can make them easier to purchase and get into the market. For investors who are just starting out and who don't have a lot of capital to invest, this can be an option to look at. Of course, like any type of investment, there are benefits and negatives to working with penny stocks. The biggest advantage here though is that these are more affordable, making it easier for investors to get started.

There are also some issues that show up when it comes to the value of a company that offers penny stocks. If you see any negative movements in the stock, even if the movement is small, this can make a big impact on the type of return that you can get. Many times, the trades that are done on the penny stocks won't be regulated unlike with the traditional stock market, so you will have a lot more risk if you trade here.

If you are still interested in looking at penny stocks and seeing what they have to offer, it is important to be careful and really analyze a company before you get started. Some of the guidelines that you should consider following to get the best results are as follows:

• Always read the warnings that are provided by the regulators.
• Do your own background check on the company.
• Make sure that the penny stock is really what you want to work with.
• Make sure that you understand how much disclosure the company is giving you and if this is really the best method to use.

Each of the trading options that we have talked about in this chapter will provide varying amounts of risks that you will need to consider before starting. All of them have the potential to help you earn money; you just need to learn how they work and pick the one that is right for you. One of the great things about investing in the stock market though is that you get the option to work on many different types of stocks, rather than just being stuck with one option when picking out your type of investment. You can try out a few different things and see what ends up working out the best for you!

Chapter 5: How to Know When a Stock Is Right for You?

There are a lot of stock types that you can choose from when you first get started. However, with all of these options, you may not be sure where to start. Remember here that you shouldn't just rush in and pick the first stock that you see. You must go through and do a full analysis of several stocks to make sure that you pick out a good one that will earn you some profits and one that will work with the strategy that you want to go with.

If you have already done some research and you have a list of companies you are interested in working with, the next step is to go to the website of these companies and see if they list out any information about their stocks. Look for financial reports at this time as well as any other information that will help you to get a good idea of how the company is doing. The more information you can gather about the company, the better decisions you can make when you decide to invest.

Of course, you want to make sure that you choose an investment that will do well if you want to make money. This helps your peace of mind so that you know the investment will not go to waste and you can get a return that is worth your time. Some of the factors that you should look for when determining how well a company is doing include:

- The profit margin of that company
- The return on equity for that company
- The past performance as well as the expected growth
- The debts that the company currently has
- The debt to equity ratio: This means that you would take the debt of the company and divide it by the equity of the shareholders. If this is a low number, it is a safer investment.

Things to Look for with a Company

When you first get started in the stock market, you may wonder what companies are the best to work with. While it is tempting for a beginner to just rush into the market and grab a few stocks that seem good on the surface, it is important for you to stop and look at the company as a whole to make sure that it is the right choice for you.

Some of the different factors that you should look into when picking out a company to invest in includes:

• How the Business Management Works

This is a very important thing to consider when investing because the management of the business can really help you figure out how well the company will do in the future. While you probably won't be able to go in directly and meet the people who manage the business, there are a few signs that you should look out for to make sure the management acts in a way that will help the business to grow.

One place to look is at the return on equity for the business, as well as how much income current shareholders can earn each year. If you notice that the return on equity is a minimum of 5%, then this is a good investment to work with.

• Stocks from a Good Business Sector

The industry that you choose to invest in is also important. You will quickly find that some industries will be better investments of your time compared to others, and there are even some industries that seem to be more volatile. The way that you choose to invest can depend on these factors along with how much money you have available and more.

As an investor, you may choose to go with just one business sector and invest your money, or you may decide to spread it out and grow your portfolio between more than one industry. The latter is often the best to grow out your portfolio because it ensures that you take on less risk and won't lose everything if one investment goes down. But for some new investors, it may only be possible to invest in one industry in the beginning. If the latter is right for you, make sure that you pick out a good sector to work with.

- Growing Profits

As a new investor, you must make sure that you pick out a company that is already bringing in profits. A company that not only brings in a profit, but shows a growing profit from one year to the next can be even better—companies that show a steady share growth that is at least 5% or more. This is a great way to keep your investment safe when you first start and can ensure that you will bring in at least a little bit of profit, even as a beginner.

- The Size of a Company

Even if the company is doing well, it is going to be riskier to invest in if it is a smaller company, especially when compared to some larger ones. The larger companies have been in the market for some, and therefore have been able to establish themselves a bit better. They have proven that they can deal with tough economic times or other issues that can be hard for a smaller business.

Many beginners will start with larger companies because it takes less risk to get started. Then, after they get into the market and learn a bit more, they will take risks and work with the smaller companies. But for someone who is brand new to this investment type, it is much better to work with bigger companies because you know they can handle any changes that may come up.

- Manageable Debt

It is going to be nearly impossible to find a company to trade with that doesn't have any debts. That is not the biggest concern when you take a look at a company. Instead, you need to find out how the company manages their debt, how much debt they have, and the ratio of debt to income for that company. The answers to these questions can greatly influence whether the company is a good investment or not.

If you notice that the company has a lot of debt, especially when compared to their profits, this can be bad news for you. This means that more of their profits need to go to paying off their debts, rather than paying the shareholder's dividend payments each quarter. And if the company is not able to handle their debts very well, they may continue to take on too much debt. Over time, they will go under, and you will end up losing out as well. A good rate to look for to know that the company can handle their debts is .5%of debt per capital to keep you safe.

• Dividend Payments

Companies that can return some of their profits to the investors are some of the best to choose to go with. This basically means that you will be able to make money with that company. The company can manage their money well enough that they can pay their workers, their debts, and anything else, and then still have enough left over to pay their investors as well.

When you take a look at a company, it is a good idea to consider the size of the dividend payment that you will receive. You want to make sure that you earn at least 2% so that you can get some of your investment back. If you want to turn the stock market into a full-time income, you will want to aim more for businesses that offer 6% or higher. But as a beginner trader, the 2-3% is usually going to be enough.

• Stocks with Enough Liquidity

This is important because you want to make sure that you can get something when you sell the stock. The ones that are considered liquid are the stocks that you are easily able to sell because there are some buyers for it. If you decide for some reason that you want to get out of the stock market, you want it to be liquid enough that you can sell it later. There are a few stocks that are not that liquid, and it is going to be a lot of work to try to sell them, which can cost you a lot of money if the market goes down at some time. Consider going with some stocks that will allow you to sell them fast if you find that the need does arise.

As you can see, you will need to take the time to really look at all of the aspects of a company to see if it is going to be a good investment to help you out. You should take a look at all of these aspects when it comes to which companies you would like to invest in because it will help you to know if it is healthy or if some issues will arise with your earnings. If you can do this complete analysis, it is going to be much easier or you to get the return on investment that you want.

Chapter 6: Option Trading Strategies

Options trading in the realm of the stock market has a lot of play potential, and it is loaded with money-related advantages when you pick and pursue the correct strategy. There are numerous option trading strategies that a financial specialist can choose from. Contingent upon the impression you have about the course of stock value development, you can select an options strategy.

There are a few strategies for trading options that are utilized for the most part, for example, bullish, bearish, and impartial procedures. If you have an impression of the stock cost going in any case, at that point, bullish or bearish strategies are utilized. If you have no idea about the stock value development, at that point, the nonpartisan approach is the correct strategy to pick.

When you expect the hidden stock cost going up, then the bullish strategy ought to be utilized. Anyway, with this strategy, it is urgent to analyze the sum that the stock cost can increment and the period in which the rally will happen. This examination will assist the trader in picking the best trading strategy. The absolute most common bullish option trading strategies utilized in the stock market are the call buying strategy, the bull put spread, bull call spread, short put strategy, the long call, the secured call, the defensive put, and the collar strategy. The call buying strategy is the most bullish strategy through the bull put spread, and bull call spreads are the cheap ones. With this strategy, you would make money as long as the stock cost does not go somewhere around the termination date.

If you hypothesize that the original stock cost will have a descending pattern, then bearish options trading strategy, which is the inverse to the bullish strategy is the correct one to pick. On account of the bearish strategy, it is essential to comprehend the dimension and furthermore the time allotment at which the costs of a stock will tumble to pick the best trading strategy. A portion of the commonly executed bearish strategies are a short call, long put, short manufactured, set back spread, call bear spread, and put bear spread. The most bearish options trading strategy among all is the put buying strategy which is drilled generally by tenderfoots in this field. The call bear spread and the put bear spread are the unassumingly bearish choices procedures.

When you are oblivious concerning the improvement of the crucial stock esteem, at that point, you should pick an unprejudiced alternative exchanging procedure which is generally called a non-directional exchanging methodology. The potential advantage depends upon the unsteadiness of the underlying stock expense. Some regular cases of impartial trading systems are straddle and butterfly.

In straddle system, you would purchase or sell alternative backups. Right when the merchant purchases the subordinate, at that point it is known as a long straddle while when the broker sells the auxiliary, it is known as a short straddle. Butterfly procedure is less hazardous alternatives exchanging methodology. This system incorporates two positions, the long butterfly position, and the short butterfly position. At the point when the future instability is lower than the suggested unpredictability then you would make benefit in a long butterfly though, in a short butterfly, you make a benefit when the future instability of the underlying stock is higher than the inferred variability of the capital.

Other than these two unbiased strategies, there are different commonly utilized strategies, for example, choke, guts, chance inversion, and condor.

There are numerous online projects and instructional classes that will show you how to trade options and pick the correct strategy that would accommodate your objectives and trading style.

Why Use Option Trading Strategies?

Numerous open door searchers are pulled in to options trading as they have heard stories making guarantees of quick benefits. The issue is that these traders come in considering nothing more than stuffing their financial balances loaded with money in a short timeframe. While this situation is reachable, the chances are positively going admirably against you. As a rule, accomplishing considerable benefits in a short timespan includes an incredibly high hazard options trading strategy. The way to your prosperity is finding a solid plan and acing it. It is much better to pull off substantial gains instead of attempting to hit a grand slam. When you know one strategy, well you can learn others.

The following are a portion of the options trading strategies that you may consider.

Mainstream strategies to trade options include:

- Bullish on instability
- Bearish on instability
- Selling Credit Spreads
- Bearish strategies
- Selling Covered Calls
- Bullish strategies
- Nonpartisan or non-directional strategies
- Date-book Straddle
- Chokes

The above rundown is not the slightest bit a thorough rundown; there are a lot of different strategies that you may utilize. The motivation behind this section is to give you a little taste of a portion of the potential outcomes. Underneath I develop a couple.

Selling Credit Spreads - If you are searching for a strategy that does not include wedding your stock options profession, at that point, this is one you could consider. There is nothing worse than following a procedure that expects you to screen the market for each moment of the trading day. You can finish what is included with this strategy in around an hour a week, and whenever done effectively, you may probably build your portfolio by approximately 10-15 percent month to month. They are incredible returns that truly put to disgrace what the banks are putting forth. To execute this strategy, you have to realize how to complete a pattern investigation on the market. The extent of this part does not enable me to cover this further. You are best encouraged to join the mailing list on this site.

Bullish Strategy - If you are expecting the hidden stock of an option to expand, then you could go with this strategy. The Bullish options trading strategies are brought into play when you, as the trader anticipates that the underlying stock cost should increment in esteem. You have to consider precisely how high the stock cost is probably going to go and inside what time span. The in all probability strategy decision for a bullish trader is a basic call-buying strategy. This is very mainstream with fledglings. Other bullish strategies incorporate Covered Straddle, Bull Calendar Spread and The Collar.

Complex Strategies - These incorporate such things as iron condors, butterflies, straddles, and chokes. Exactly where do they think of the names utilized in strategies for options trading? Bizarre right? The ones I have recorded here whenever pursued effectively are commonly okay while in the meantime, is almost sure to be beneficial. The detriment is that they are costly, either because of the way that you are trading expensive options or on account of high brokerage expenses which come to fruition because of the number of trades included.

You ought to recall that options are very versatile trading instruments. With such extraordinary adaptability, this is the place numerous individuals miss the point. They feel that the more complicated an options trading strategy is, the more fruitful it very well may be. Indeed it very well may be a remarkable inverse. The more complicated, the more open you could be to hazard while in the meantime, constraining benefit potential.

Likewise, with any strategy, you utilize with your options trading business and approach it with deference. Try not to trade live until you have given it a decent test using a training account. At precisely that point should you consider running with it using your actual money?

When figuring out how to trade options, it is continually fitting to utilize chance capital when trading with actual money possibly. This implies probably use money that you can stand to lose when you have trades that conflict with you. There you go that contacts the outside of options trading strategies. You will need to find out more and after that, select a plan to trade your options utilizing a test account. From that point who knows?

Continuously recollect not to give things a chance to escape hand. If you are learning a new strategy, trade with one contract at any given moment. If you go over the edge, you will before long end up crazy and headed towards catastrophe. Options trading isn't a race. You have time on your side, and you should take advantage of it. The market will at present be here tomorrow.

How to Choose the Best Options Trading Strategy

The enchantment of options trading is that it takes into consideration an assortment of procedures to be coordinated with various stock trading methods of insight. Every strategy has an alternate benefit and hazard resistance level, and utilizing a variety of techniques can zest up a portfolio in all respects pleasantly! In this part, I will lay out four different stock trading techniques, and how they can be coordinated with relating options trading systems which you can apply to your portfolio. The principal, though, is to concentrate on an underlying stock trading strategy initially, and after that, add critical influence and capacity to the trade by utilizing options.

The most significant factor while considering every one of these methodologies is the idea of TIME DECAY. The estimation of any choice decays after some time, until the day the alternative lapses. This idea can be the significant enemy of any alternative trade, eating into its profits, or it very well may be the way to successful and gainful choice trading.

Right off the bat, which Strategy?

There are commonly four unique systems utilized by stock traders, every one of which has suggestions when connected to options:

(I) Position Trading

Merchants purchase a stock and hold it for extended timeframes, in light of good basics of the organization. They will regularly trust that a share will achieve high esteem, and afterward watch for institutional or insider buying before making a move. As the stock cost builds, they pay a unique mind to different buyers to venture in and move the price much further.

Proper OPTION STRATEGY

Buying calls and puts aren't proper, because you pay enormous premiums for time esteem, the vast majority of which could be cleared out after some time even as the stock gains in cost. TIME DECAY is your enemy.

Selling covered calls every month in the choice cycle on the stock you effectively possess can substantially decrease the cost you paid for the stock in the leading trade. Regardless of whether the stock goes down, you can even now turned out a champ!

(ii) Momentum or Trend trading

When a stock has clarified move or breakout, the Momentum traders venture in and ride the share up along a pattern to its first significant inversion. They would like to make shorter-term profits from a quick move in the cost. Holding periods go from about a month and a half to a half year.

Suitable OPTION STRATEGY

Buying calls and puts aren't fitting, since you pay enormous premiums for time esteem, a large portion of which will be cleared out after some time even as the stock gains in cost. TIME DECAY is your enemy with Momentum Trading, except if you have an exceptionally robust and quick moving pattern.

Selling Credit Spreads is a decent strategy, and in reality can be genuinely productive, in light of the fact that as you sell spreads on the contrary leg from the stock's heading of force (for example selling put acknowledge spreads in stock for an emphatically bullish pattern), you can more than once buy back the ranges for least expense and sell another range nearer in. This strategy can without much of a stretch return 10-15% benefit every month. Time Decay is your distinct advantage for trading this strategy.

Selling Naked Puts is a decent strategy, and can be significantly more productive than selling credit spreads. It leaves you a place of perhaps purchasing a lot of stock if the trade conflicts with you, thus your broker expects you to have a lot of edges.

(iii) Swing Trading

Swing Traders buy and sell swings or motions inside a pattern. Holding times are from somewhere in the range of 2 and ten days. This is a shorter term trading method that is more reliant on the pattern bearing than it is on essentials or specialized pointers.

Suitable OPTION STRATEGY

If you have aced the aptitude of recognizing inversions or swings inside a pattern, and ability to design a leave strategy, you will most likely begin buying calls and puts, or DITM options, which will take you to substantial profits! With Swing Trading, holding times are short (2-10 days) thus you limit the impact of your most despised enemy, TIME DECAY.

(iv) Day Trading

Informal investors center around the many little moves that occur amid the trading day, for the most part, appeared by candle designs. This strategy has a broker's requirement of at least $25,000 to qualify, which thumps out numerous learners.

Suitable OPTION STRATEGY

Choice trading isn't fitting with this strategy. Broker charges for options trading are very high, and Day Traders end up paying considerable entireties to their brokers.

Characterizing Your Trade Success Through Your Options Trading Strategies

Would you like to make each progression of your trading procedure a beyond any doubt shot towards your trade success? Do you wish to dispense with or, if not, reduce your stresses over your trade commitment and become progressively particular about your trade execution? Is it accurate to say that you are in for something which could enable you to improve as an entertainer in the options trading industry? When you got 'yes' as your response to those inquiries, this part is something for you that will give you a few bits of advice about your trade. With this, you should concentrate on your options trading techniques.

Tossing Sure Shots

A trader's strategy in options trading is incredible assistance in making his trade progress. This strategy could characterize the trader himself when he ends up victorious or not. Having significant procedures resembles having an endowment of foreseeing what will occur later on in which the trader must be set up to stay away from misfortunes concerning his trade. With the assistance of these procedures that the trader utilizes, each progression that the trader will perform will bolster his objectives and set up his arrangements for the future conditions which may happen that will shake his trade execution. With that, there will be an affirmation that the trader will toss beyond any doubt shots and make the most of the scoreboard for him.

Lesser Worries

Choice trading is a simple sort of trade wherein a trader could have lesser stresses concerning misfortunes that he may look amid his trade commitment. The pressure that you may be understanding because of the business stresses that accidents may give you has an alleviation in options trading through your options trading systems. We can't state that misfortunes can be completely disposed of in light of the fact that

that will be unthinkable, however you can make sure that they might be cut down in the event that you have that great strategy, since it will give you a few thoughts of what may occur amid your trade commitment which will assist you with becoming much arranged. This will help you with stopping stressing and become quiet in sitting tight for your great benefit toward the finish of each commitment that you will make.

Better Performance

To whole it up, having beyond any doubt shots and fewer stresses in your trade execution will help you in up-evaluating yourself as a superior trader and help you acquire from options trading. On account of your techniques which fill in as high instruments which will give you certainty about your success in all commitment that you will make. These successes will open you more opportunities that you may snatch, which will offer you higher benefit than what you anticipate. This is proof that choice trading is a commendable field which is flooding with success opportunities for financial specialists who get into it. Also, this likewise demonstrates trading with methodologies is an extraordinary activity to have a beyond any doubt success.

Finding your options trading procedures isn't that difficult, notwithstanding for a novice in this field. It is a simple task to perform because it is you who knows your trade high. Thinking about its qualities and shortcomings, you would almost certainly determine what you ought to do to improve the great and adapt up to the terrible. It is likewise extraordinary assistance if you will discover something to peruse or watch concerning procedures in this field with the end goal for you to get learning and understanding that will fill in as excellent guides in your techniques. With this, options trading will wind up more straightforward and increasingly beneficial for you. Good karma!

How to Discover Options Trading Strategies You Can Use

Options trading strategies exist since somebody had the warning to make options on stocks, ETF's, files, and so forth. Anybody, even a fledgling trader, can utilize one of the many trading strategies to play the underlying security.

The fact of the matter is a trader can be on the two sides of the market in the meantime with a portion of these strategies. They can be wagering specific security will go one way while supporting that with a position that says it will go the other way.

In some cases, you as the trader, can be the person who takes in the alternative premium by primarily selling that specific choice. If you become the seller, you trust the underlying security will go the contrary way, and you won't just have the option to take the top-notch sum yet you won't need to pay out should you be on the wrong side.

Understanding this style of trading is vital before you enter the diversion. If you don't have the foggiest idea about a fundamental put or call from an opening in the ground, you most likely shouldn't be in the diversion. You are possibly asking to lose money if you don't comprehend in any event the essentials of options trading.

On account of this thing called the Internet, an options trader can do what is usually called online options trading. The trader still uses a trading house, for example, a built-up full-time broker; however, as opposed to going into a block and mortar office, the trader executes the trade on his PC.

A standout amongst the ideal approaches to comprehend and find trading strategies you can utilize is to visit a few options trading or potentially data destinations and read all that they distribute on options. For instance, if you need to take the premium and still support your position, you may complete a credit spread.

This specific spread enables you to make money selling a choice of particular security while buying a decision on this equivalent security yet farther in time. Should what I just said sound like an unknown dialect, don't stress over it. Your examination will have vast amounts of models.

Most online brokerage houses have an options division dedicated to clarifying options, talking about stock options trading, proposing specific options trading frameworks and that's just the beginning. They will probably furnish you the trader with as much learning about the product as they can. They need you to trade through them so they can profit by the commissions earned.

When you are unfriendly to start your adventure to finding choice trading strategies through brokerage houses, web indexes offer various options. Options trading strategies will turn out to be second nature to the trader who is resolved to learning this quick-paced and energizing venture vehicle.

What Are the Different Options Trading Strategies?

Options are truly adaptable and no-commitment money related instruments used to benefit from various market conditions or potentially to constrain trading dangers and presentation. Options strategies are techniques to accomplish clear options trading objectives and to all the more likely use multiple chances and market conditions. Not at all like most other money-related instruments have options empowered traders to benefit from any market conditions even in quick downtrends and in no price changes.

There are various options trading strategies accessible now, and new ones are concocted ordinary. Some of them are generally well known and pursued; however, some others are trading secrets of specific people or gatherings. There are no strategies to benefit from each market condition; in certainty for successful implementation, the vast majority of them require a few essentials. Options trading strategies can be necessary, which need typical trading stages and incorporate a couple of agreements/traders OR can be perplexing, which require complex trading frameworks and includes numerous agreements/trades.

Contingent upon nature and implementation, options trading strategies can be arranged to 3 fundamental gatherings as,

1. Bullish: These are strategies which are used when the underlying product price is relied upon to go up. As it were the successful implementation requires a price increase of the underlying product. Precedents incorporate short put, long call, engineered large stock, bull spread, and so forth.

2. Bearish: These are used when the underlying product price is relied upon to go down, and successful implementation requires price decline. Precedents incorporate long put, short call, bear spread, engineered short stock, and so on.

3. Non-Directional or Market Neutral: These strategies are used on expected price instability of the underlying instrument and are not rely upon high price points and low points. Accomplishment with these is accomplished when the regular price change is achieved or not performed. Precedents incorporate straddles, chokes, butterfly, and so forth. Non-directional strategies can be additionally separated into two as bullish-on-instability and bearish-on-unpredictability.

Notwithstanding the over three principle classifications two different classifications additionally exist which are occasion-driven, and stock-mix strategies; the previous expects/considers a particular time like mergers and takeovers and endeavor to benefit from that and the later is mind-boggling strategies that incorporate blends of trades or choice sorts.

No single options trading strategy suits each trader. Indeed the correct decision ought to rely upon numerous variables like the underlying product, market conditions and instability, trader experience, access to cites and modern trading frameworks, brokerage administration trader utilizing, trader portfolio size and hazard resistance, long-term or short-term trading objectives, and money the executives. Albeit, a significant number of the present trading frameworks are pre-stacked to help numerous well-known strategies it is an excellent plan to learn however many strategy as could be expected and to make them effectively open to you. The general suggestion is that to actualize basic one when you are a novice and change to increasingly complex ones as you become more acquainted with progressively about various options, the market, and its developments.

The Use of Options Trading Strategies

Do you have stresses concerning by what means will you reduce the dangers of your commitment in options trading? If you are wishing of having lesser misfortune and higher benefit? Would you like to augment your assets and develop your prosperity rate? If your answer is 'yes,' all you need is a compelling and proficient options trading strategy. This will be such a significant amount of supportive for novices, specialists, and different dimensions of people who are taking part in the options trading business.

It is hugely a reason for cerebral pain to consider how much benefit you are missing a result of the misfortunes happening amid your exchanges. The facts demonstrate that dangers are always present in all undertakings, yet a lot of it isn't reliable. You may not dispense with them. However you can even now accomplish something and that its to limit them by utilizing strategies.

Strategies to be utilized to develop your trade are resolved as ahead of schedule as you're arranging stage. These are generally insignificant products of a decent arrangement which is embraced all together for a trader to seek after his objectives and targets. In the phase of arranging, you will initially consider "what would you like to do?" at that point you will figure "In what manner will you do it?" that is how you will decide the ways on the best way to make your trade successful.

Options trading strategies are the determinants of your trade movement. It will be your device is moving, which can be contrasted and a mixing wheel of a vehicle. These strategies will enable you to decide whether your alternative will move evenly, vertically, or corner to corner. The inquiry is the thing that strategy is the best.

When you are allowed to ask every one of the people who are encountering accomplishment in options trading on what strategy they are utilizing, you may get a couple of answers as well as a wide assortment. That is because there is no such thing as a "one size fits all" strategy in this field. It will be progressively compelling in the event that you will alter your very own policy dependent on your arrangement in light of the fact that as a trader you are the person who splendidly knows every one of the qualities and shortcoming of your trade so you can decide precisely what will be the best strategy that will be useful for you.

Another significant thing in deciding your strategy is that you should initially know the fundamentals. Most procedures are only blends of the four essential trades, in particular: long call, long put, short call, and shot put. This necessary information will help decide you're modified powerful and proficient strategy. You are allowed to pick what you think will support you.

As a trader who needs achievement in the field of options, trading must resemble a chess player. Options trading, similar to chess, are a battle of strategies; the individuals who will have the beyond any doubt win are the individuals who are having their best options trading strategies. You should remember that your every move will have a significant effect in the entire fight; all things considered, you should turn out to be careful in your every step. Ensure that you will do is dependable for the success and won't be the purpose behind you to misfortune.

Chapter 7: Trading Strategies – Stocks, ETFs

If you have a substantial amount of capital and you have mastered the technique of being patient, then you can get started in stock trading. However, the secret to becoming a successful stock trader requires that you reduce losses while you search for good trade setups that have a favorable risk. Although it appears smooth to get into the business, there are a few steps that you should be ready to follow. If you jump quickly into stock trading without following these steps, you may end up losing most of your money.

Well, let us look at the steps of becoming a Stock trader.

Get a Demo Account

A Stock trading demo account is one with monopoly money in it and linked to the live market. In a demo account, you can place trades in real time and represent what would be true if the money was real.

Before you can take part in the actual trade, you'll need practice. A demo account will grant you the ability to practice trading with no pressure. Once you have opened several trades and mastered a few skills in Stock trading, you'll be ready to move to the next step.

Finding Profit targets on your trade

Before you can switch to live trading and money on the line, you must be able to trade on your demo account profitably. Make sure that your track record should be more than a few weeks, preferably six months.

It will be hard to stop trading once you make the first few profitable trades, but the experience is vital in Stock trading. It's something that has no shortcut; you will need to get it through hard work.

How you can practice Stock Trading before going Live

Besides opening virtual trades on the demo account, find out some trading advice from a Stock trainer. As a trader, you must come up with your style of trading, but at the start, it is essential to have a professional trainer to give you directions and advice. Stock trading may appear tough in the early days and with some guidance, it can be easy and profitable.

What is a share?

If you own a share, it means that you own a portion of an organization. It is the same way you can visualize your ownership of a company as a slice of bread cut out from a loaf of bread. A person who owns shares is known as a shareholder. A shareholder is entitled to receiving cash flows; cash flow is also known as a dividend. Dividends are given by an organization when its board of directors declares that the company has made sufficient profits to distribute to the shareholders. Board of directors also own shares in the company. In most cases, you may find that the board of directors holds a majority of the shares of the company.

Owning a share is important because it gives you the right to cast a vote on the decisions of the organization. A share can also be called stock or equity.

What does the share price mean?

The share price is the price at which a particular stock can be sold or bought in the market. The value of the share price is influenced by many factors such as supply and demand for a specific organization's shares.

Factors influencing the stock price

If a company has more buyers than sellers of its shares, the share prices will increase because the demand is high. Demand and supply are inversely proportional. That is to say that when the demand is high, the supply is low and vice versa.

When the sellers are more than buyers for a specific organization's shares, stock prices usually reduce because there are more of these equities available.

If a company makes a lot of profits, its share will be more valuable because a majority of people believe that investing with the company will yield gains.

Political and economic factors also affect the price of stocks in the market.

How do I make a decision on which company to invest?

It is advisable for you to research the stock market by reading financial information regularly, seeking an opinion from a qualified expert such as a stockbroker, and attending investment courses.

You can also assess the performance of the company by studying analyst reports and reading the company's financial statements. By doing this, you will have a higher chance of making educated decisions on the companies to invest your hard-earned funds.

Decide on how much risk you are willing to take, the amount of profit you expect, and the investment instruments that meet your requirements. You can consult a qualified expert if you need extra advice.

Commit to your investment objective. Always bear in mind that investing for the long run is advisable. For example, you should have a 5 –year investment objective.

Decide on how long you can wait for returns and be patient. If the stock you invest in fails to perform for a year, you may need to change your strategy by choosing another stock.

Invest with funds you are willing to lose and that you do not require in the short run. That is, make sure you have disposable funds after taking care of all your daily expenses.

You should be aware that investing can help you make additional income, but there is also a risk of losing funds in the short run.

Types of Stocks and Investment products

There are different types of investment products and shares that may suit your needs. They are categorized into two groups: safe (conservative) shares and risky shares. The following is a list of investment products:

N-Ordinary shares

B-Ordinary shares

Preference shares

Ordinary shares

Exchange Traded Funds

RISK

A risk is a term that means the likelihood of losing all or part of your initial investment, or making fewer profits than you had expected. Different investment products and securities have different levels of risk. Low-risk securities are listed below:

Exchange-traded fund (ETFs)

It is an investment product that is traded on share exchanges just like stocks. ETFs hold assets such as commodities, stocks, and bonds. It operates with an arbitrage technique designed to make it trade close to its average asset value. However, deviations can occur most of the time.

Money in a bank account that earns interest annually.

Bonds

A bond is an interest-earning debt financial instrument issued by a government. The redemption period for government bonds is usually one or more years after issuance.

Higher risk securities are listed below:

• Warrants

• Shares

• Corporate bonds, and

• Derivatives

Stock investment is riskier than some other investments. The main reason for this is because stock prices fall and rise all the time due to political and economic factors that affect the market forces. However, the higher the risk involved the greater the possibility of making profits. Usually, higher risk means a higher return on investment.

Is it possible to minimize the risk of my investment?

Yes, you may minimize your exposure by diversifying your investment. Diversification means investing in a variety of financial instrument such as stocks, bonds, commodities, et cetera. It is common knowledge that putting all your "eggs" in one "basket" will result in a more significant exposure and hence higher chances of losing. You should make it your priority to choose investments from different sectors, investment products, and organizations. To diversify your portfolio correctly, you may need to seek advice from a qualified expert such as a stockbroker, reading financial books and news, and attending investment courses.

Is it challenging to manage my investment portfolio?

Certain financial investment instruments need little or no management. In spite of this, you should be aware of how your investments are faring on. Stockbrokers provide certain services to help you manage your stock investments. These services include:

● Non-discretionary

In this type of service, all investment decisions are made by the stock trader after receiving necessary advice from the stockbroker.

● Discretionary

All investment decisions are made by the stockbroker without necessarily consulting with the investor, but it is made according to the agreed investment objectives.

Seasoned and experienced investors can use a single financial instrument that provides exposure to different shares, commodities, and bonds. This instrument is called Exchange Traded Fund.

ETFs are easy to research as compared to researching many companies. They are less cheap to maintain and help you spread your risk across different trading instruments. On the other hand, ETFs do not give you direct voting right as is the case with ordinary stocks. Another benefit of ETFs is that they earn dividends at the end of the investment period.

Do I require a lot of funds to begin investing in stocks?

You do not need a lot of funds to invest in the stock market because there are numerous financial products available to cater to everyone's capability. Some products such as ETFs provide investment offers where a debit order can be made every month or a lump sum payment made at once.

Stockbrokers do not always need a minimum amount of money for investment. With the availability of online share trading, you may invest any amount of money on stocks through the internet. Nonetheless, you should be informed that stockbrokers do charge a certain amount of fees for their services. You should invest an amount of money where the fees charged are less than the amount you have invested.

How can I access the stock market?

To sell or purchase shares on the stock market you need to register for an account with one of the available stockbrokers such as etoro.com. Buying and selling ETFs do not require you to have an account with a stockbroker. You may talk to ETF providers directly to invest in such investment products. However, owning a brokerage account is essential because it gives you the option of investing in all types of investment instruments.

Important points to consider

Invest a reasonable amount of money in comparison to the number of fees you will pay the stockbroker.

Exercise self-discipline by committing to a long-term investment approach, and always monitor the performance of your investment.

Be patient by ensuring that you are not emotionally attached to your investment. Every trading day is different. You may make profits on some days and also lose on other days. Make sure your investment strategy is profitable in the long-run.

See to it that your investment portfolio is diversified.

Do not borrow funds to invest, mainly if you are unsure whether you will make enough profits to repay the loan.

Online Trading

It refers to buying and selling stocks or other assets by the use of a broker's internet-based website or trading platform. Currencies, futures, options, ETFs, mutual funds, bonds, and stocks can all be traded online. It is called self-directed investing or e-trading.

As mentioned above, in a split of a second you can trade stocks and other financial instruments such as the Dollar or Euro, some commodities such as Gold or Oil as well as main market indices.

One more advantage of online trading is that the improvement in the rate of which trades can be implemented and settled, since there is no demand for paper-based files to be reproduced, registered and entered into a digital format. Once an investor opens a buy position on the internet, the trade is set in a database that assesses for the very best price by searching all of the marketplace trades that trade the inventory in the investor's currency. The market with the very best price fits the buyer with a vendor and sends the confirmation to the purchaser's agent and the seller's agent. All this process can be achieved within minutes of opening a trade, in comparison to making a telephone call that requires several confirmation steps before the representative can input the purchase.

It is all up to investors or stock traders to do their research about a broker before opening trading accounts with the business. Before an account is opened, the customer will be requested to complete a questionnaire about their investment and financial history to ascertain which sort of trading accounts is acceptable for the customer. On the flip side, an experienced trader who would love to execute various trading strategies will be provided with a margin account where he can purchase, brief, and compose securities such as shares, options, futures, and currencies.

Not all securities are all readily available to be traded on the internet, depending upon your broker. Some agents need you to call them to put a transaction on any shares trading on the pink sheets and choose stocks trading over-the-counter. Additionally, not all agents ease derivatives trading in currencies and commodities throughout their affiliate platforms. Because of this, it's necessary that the dealer knows what a broker offers before registering with the trading platform.

Most online trading classes are centered on instructing marketplace mechanisms and technical evaluation, while others might concentrate on more specific strategies or particular asset classes. Courses may offer a comprehensive summary of technical analysis in addition to other strategies designed for specific asset classes. They assist traders quickly reach a stage where they are comfortable creating approaches and executing trades.

Online trading classes often offer a collection of video or text courses to present theories in addition to one-on-one or group training to assist in reinforcing these concepts. Live marketplace sessions might also be provided to reveal trading techniques in practice.

Portfolio Management

Portfolio management means the collection of securities and continuous shifting of the portfolio in the light of changing the attractiveness of the components of their portfolio.

It is a choice of revising the range of securities while considering all the characteristics of an investor. Portfolio management comprises portfolio preparation, selection, and structure, evaluation, and review of securities. The ability in portfolio management is located in achieving a sound balance between the aims of security, liquidity, and profitability.

Timing is an essential aspect of portfolio management. Ideally, investors must sell at market tops and purchase at market bottoms. Investors can change from bonds to discuss within a bullish market and vice-versa at a bearish market. Portfolio management is about strengths, weaknesses, opportunities, and dangers in the selection of debt vs. equity, national vs. international, expansion vs. security, and several other challenges encountered in the effort to maximize returns at a specific desire for risk.

Portfolio management refers to the choice of securities and their constant shifting from the portfolio to maximize the yields to match the specific objectives of the investor. However, it requires experience in choosing the ideal combination of securities in altering marketplace conditions to get the most out of this stock exchange. In India, in addition to in several western nations, portfolio management agency has assumed the function of technical support, and several of expert merchant bankers compete aggressively to supply the very best to wealthy customers, who have very little time to handle their investments. The concept is catching up with the boom at the capital market, and an increasing number of traders are likely to make the profits from their hard-earned savings.

Chapter 8: Bonds

A bond is a type of loan which is taken out by companies for various reasons. The money is given by the investors who aim to get some level of interest from the same company. Therefore, the return obtained from investing in bonds is the interest paid for the use of the money. As with any other investment, the more money you put into the purchase of bonds, the higher the interest payable is at the end of a financial period.

Bonds specify the amount borrowed and the date at which the bond will be paid back. The payback date is known as the maturity date, and the investors receive their money in full. Before the maturity date arrives, the shareholders are subject to be paid progressive interest. For instance, an investor may take a $1000 bond with a maturity date of 10 years. Assuming the bond pays an interest of 5% per annum, the shareowner is bound to receive $50 in interest every year until the maturity date comes, then he or she gets his or her initial investment of $1000 back.

Many investors assert bonds are among the safest investments to make since it ensures they will get back their principal amount after maturity. In addition to the initial investment amount being reimbursed, the investors benefit from interests paid progressively. Nevertheless, it is important to understand an investor takes a bond and hopes the company will be able to make enough money to pay interests, as well as refund the initial capital after the maturity period. Unlike stocks where the stockholders become partial owners of a company, bond owners are just lenders who do not own any stakes in it.

Benefits of Investing in Bonds

Like any other investment, there are advantages and disadvantages which the bond owners accrue. These are some of those benefits.

A regular source of income

Depending on the agreement signed between the company and the lender, interest payments are rendered after a certain period. The company is obliged to pay out the interests as agreed upon and without fail every financial period. For this reason, the investors are always assured of a steady source of income at different payment times.

Preference during bankruptcy

There are instances when a company goes bankrupt due to various reasons. In the case of such an occurrence, the bondholders are usually given the first preference in payment. Preferential treatment makes them safer sources of investment.

Notably, bonds are either secured or unsecured. The unsecured bonds are referred to as debentures, and the interest payment and return of the principal amount are determined by the issuing company. In case of bankruptcy, the bondholders are given the first priority, although it is never a guarantee they will get all of their investment back

Secured bonds are the most preferred type of bond since they are attached to assets pledged by the company in case it fails. Therefore, the investors are guaranteed of getting back all of their initial investment even when the company fails since the assets will be sold off.

Reduced risks

In any financial market, there is often the fluctuation of prices. It also applies in stocks, and their valuation at one time may be different at another period. Nevertheless, the fluctuation of the prices in the bond market is less prevalent and likely than in other financial markets. Therefore, the risk of losses is minimal.

Now, despite the many benefits of becoming a bond owner, there are a few disadvantages linked to the bonds market. The major disadvantage is the less upside potential. In any financial market, huge risks are always associated with huge returns. Consequently, low risks come with low returns. Bonds are considered as low-risk investments since a lender is sure to get their money back at the maturity date.

Unlike stockholders whose value in the company grows as it develops, bond investors have no stakes in the company and are only entitled to their principal amount. There is also a high risk associated with changes in interest rates. The interest rates are always subject to the economy of a country, so its depreciation will cause an overall decline in the interest amounts for the bonds. Also, the economic changes and internal issues in the company are known to cause early leaves, in which the maturity dates are brought forward. In case it occurs, an investor is refunded his or her initial investment, ultimately causing a reduction of regular income.

Finally, there is the risk of defaulted payments, in which the company fails to make payments as initially agreed upon. There are many reasons which may result in the dishonoring of the interests. They range from internal company issues to financial problems like bankruptcy. In some cases, companies may face major lawsuits, which result in their dissolvent, consequently causing the inability to honor the bond agreements.

Types of Bonds

There is an immense diversity in the bonds market, which paves the way for the creation of different types of bonds. Notably, bonds are majorly sold by large corporations, the federal government, and some government-sponsored agencies. Also, they are considered to be long-term investments since most of them mature within a range of ten to 50 years. The categories of bonds are numerous, although there are a few well-recognized types.

Treasury Bonds

Treasury bonds are marketable government securities which have a maturity of more than 10 years. They are usually issued by the federal agencies of different countries and form the largest sector of any country's bond market. The treasury bonds are among the four types of debts issued, which help in obtaining money to finance the government's spending. Any person can buy the treasury bonds, although the investment amount is considered to be immensely higher than typical financial market investments. In most cases, the minimum amount to pay for is $1000. The interests are paid regularly, either bi-annually or annually.

Among all the groups of bonds, the treasury bonds are said to give you the safest investment route. Since they are backed up by the governments in various nations, there is no risk of not being paid back. Despite the surety, though, the treasury bonds have lower interest rates than other company's bonds, making them less profitable to the investors. Most people buy them for the sole aim of using it as a hedge against instances of a market crash. They consider the money to be a part of their savings since it is kept safe even in the worst of times.

Corporate Bonds

Corporate bonds are issued by companies and organizations before getting sold to investors. Just like in treasury bonds, the corporations which provide bonds do so to be able to finance their corporate expenses. Since the bonds consist of large amounts of money, the corporations can invest them in the companies and make large profits out of them. It is the profits and returns which provide money used in the payment of interest to the investors. In the case of secured bonds, the company uses parts of its physical assets as collateral.

The corporate bonds are riskier than the treasury bonds, though. This is especially true for the unsecured bonds. Since they are not backed up by the company, the shareholders may lose their investment if bankruptcy occurs. The high risks explain the high-interest rates as corporate bonds attract more interest than treasury bonds.

Notably, corporate bonds have an almost standard coupon payment structure in all companies. The latter issues the bonds in blocks of $1000 per value. Big companies have high-value bonds, which even exceed the $100,000 mark. Similar to the treasury bonds, the investors receive interest payments until their bonds mature. You should take note of how corporations call for the prepayment of the bonds before maturity, primarily if they want to wind up the business or when the prevailing market rates are about to change. The investors may also opt to sell their bonds, most especially when there is the possibility of price movement in the market.

Municipal Bonds

The municipal bonds are issued by the local governments, from the states level down to the town and government agencies. The bonds are issued for the same reason other organizations release treasury and corporate bonds, and it is to source money for the local government.

The characteristics of the municipal bonds are also similar to the traits the treasury and corporate bonds have. The investors benefit from interest earned, which is either remitted semiannually or annually.

Investing in Bonds

Bonds are considered to be among the most lucrative investments with minimal risks. Just like the companies and government bodies involved, most people are used to borrowing money from banks and financial institutions and repaying it with interest. Institutions which offer bonds operate in a similar manner and issue interest progressively.

There are two ways through which a person can invest and make money with bonds.

• The major strategy adopted by the investors is purchasing the bonds, enjoying the interests remitted, and holding the bonds until their maturity date. Once the latter occurs, the investors can then take back their money and decide on whether to re-invest them in the same or different bonds.

• The second method is selling the bonds at a higher price than you have paid for initially. For instance, if you bought bonds worth $1000, you can sell them at $11,000 to willing investors. Most bondholders sell them off when they either want to make the quick profit or need the principal amount invested urgently. The buyers then begin enjoying the interest remitted until they mature.

Buying bonds are relatively complex since they are not publicly traded on a market exchange platform. Most of the bonds are bought over the counter or from brokers. The only bonds which are bought directly from the source are the treasury bonds since they are obtained from the government without going through a middleman. It can be problematic to purchase bonds from the middlemen since the investors are never sure if they are getting the best deal. The lack of centralization means some of the brokers may hike the prices for a few investors, and the latter might not know about it. Potential investors should understand the Financial Industry Regulatory Authority's ability to regulate the stock market through the posting of transaction prices, and the shareowners can compare them with what they are being offered.

Notably, since bonds are considered to be lower risk investments compared to stocks, it does not mean they are entirely risk-free. Some companies have defaulted payment in the past, resulting in the investors losing all of their investment amounts. Luckily, all bonds are rated from the most stable to the least. The rating is done by three major bond-rating agencies, namely S&P, Moody's, and Fitch Company. These organizations use letters, numbers or symbols to indicate the creditworthiness of the companies issuing the bonds.

S&P and Fitch use the same rating for the bonds, ranking them from the best quality to the worst. The ratings are indicated by AAA, AA, A, BBB, BB, B, CCC, CC, C, and D.

The higher the company's rating is, the more stable it is. Many investors would be cautious when buying the bonds of a company which falls below the BB rating. Those who commit a lot of money to the bonds must be careful not to lose their entire investments to low-rated companies.

Effects of Bonds in the Stock Market

Bonds and stocks are two distinct products in the financial market. The major way through which the bonds can affect the stock market is if it competes with the stocks for the investors' dollars. Therefore, many people who desire to put their money in a low-risk investment may prefer to overlook stocks and go for bonds. Despite this occurrence, when the stocks go up in value, the bonds go down, and vice versa. Investors are always likely to go for the investments which guarantee the best returns, hence the counter effect on the stocks and bonds per season.

In some rare instances, the value of both stocks and bonds can go up significantly. This often happens when there is too much money or liquidity in circulation and too few investors. In this case, the investors choose the options which are guaranteed to bring them the most returns while being relatively risk-free. Bonds are the best bet in such a market, which makes the demand for the stocks lower in comparison.

Potential investors must know the value of both stocks and bonds to be able to choose which of the investments are the best for them. The decision is dependent on two major factors, such as the shareholder's personal goal and their risk level. If you want to enjoy regular interest payments with the assurance you will get the principal amount at the end of a certain period, then the bond investment is the best for you. On the other hand, if you want a more flexible investment plan where you can buy and sell your share values easily and potentially make a lot of profits at one go, then stocks are for you. There are many day traders who have become successful in the stock market and made a huge income out of it. The investors know the risks involved since there is always a chance of losing their entire income. Nevertheless, the people who are interested in high-risk and high-returns investments are better suited for stocks.

Furthermore, investors must know how the economic cycle affects the values of both the stocks and bonds. In instances where the economy is expanding drastically, stocks are the better option due to the increased valuation. The level of risks which investors are comfortable facing is still a major factor since the stocks remain volatile regardless of the expanding economy.

Chapter 9: Finding Financial News

This chapter discusses the importance of financial news to investing in the stock market and how you can generate great returns by being armed with the right information.

As discussed earlier, there are two major approaches to investing in the stock market. First, there is the route of fundamental analysis and there is the path of technical analysis. Technical analysis involves the use of chart patterns to determine viable investment decisions. These sets of investors study the way the market has reacted in the past through the price and they make decisions as to what price would do in the future.

To explain further, a strictly technical investor/trader isn't concerned about what people are saying about the stock. His main concern is what people are doing with the stock - are they buying or selling the stock? If they are buying, he wants to know the reason. How does he find this reason? By looking at past price data with the view to understanding the psychology behind the price action.

Though you would find a lot of technical investors who read financial news and tries to factor that into their investment decisions, the truth is you could be successful in this path without paying attention to the news. The level of success you can achieve using this strategy is however subject to debate. Subsequently, if that's the kind of investor you'll like to be then this chapter might not be for you.

However, no matter your style and approach to investing, you would still find the points discussed in this chapter useful. Why? No matter how you trade, the importance of financial news cannot be over emphasized. Even a technical trader needs confirmation for any strategy he is trying to execute. He needs something outside the price action to tell him that he isn't throwing his money away. In the stock market, this edge is more often than not the difference between good and great. So even if learning about economics isn't your thing, you might need to understand the basic reaction people exhibit when the news is released. Now, let's dive into how financial news can help you achieve greatness in stock investing.

What Kind Of Financial News Are We Talking About?

If you have visited any financial website, you would have probably found that there is always too many information to comprehend per time. You also find it difficult to classify this information. So what you get at the end of the day is confusion. The reason for this is simple. Financial news website report news on all sorts of securities and asset classes so you would find information about stock, bonds, currencies, commodities, derivatives, and many more. If you don't know what to look for and why it matters, you'll be frustrated.

First, you need to understand stock information from two perspectives which we call the broad view and the narrow view. As the explanation would reveal, this is the way to analyze securities before making any decision whatsoever, you need to understand how to view financial information from this compass to make headway in the financial world.

The Broad View

Even though shares are about specific companies, those companies do not operate in a vacuum. They operate in a larger social, political and economic environment. Your focus as an investor in shares is to monitor the economic environment in which your shares operate.

For instance, if a company sells consumer product anything that makes consumers consume more or less would be relevant to their shares. Thus, information about consumer spending and inflationary pressures in the economy would be relevant to such a company. This is the importance of paying attention to the broader economic landscape when considering financial news.

Consequently, the broad view deals with information classes that affect the economy as a whole and can subsequently have an effect on shares in general or a particular class of shares. The more important information would then be – what are these kinds of information? Some of the important classes are considered below:

The General Economic Landscape

This is simply put the economics of a company. Take the United States for instance, and its economic growth rate. So let's say America is projected to grow its output by 3% this year which is higher than its 2% growth rate for the previous year. Assuming this statistic is true and you believe it to be so. Does that information tell you anything about the price of stock in the United States market for the coming year? Yes, it does.

Following from the above example, assuming you have been watching an "outsource staff" company for a while. You think the company is ripe for the taking. All their books check out and the price on the market is fair. Then, suddenly you find out that the output of the United States is projected to be better in the coming year.

How does this new information factor into your investment goals? That's simple. Increased output means that companies would definitely be looking to hire staff. Some of those staff would be from outsourcing service providers. This is good news for the prospect of your investment. This is why the broad view can never be overlooked.

But what are the specific information to look out for in this regard? They are inexhaustible but it would be prudent to discuss a few.

GDP or Growth Rate

The GDP is the total number of final goods produced in an economy over a given period of time. The information about a country's GDP gives you an indication of the economic health of any nation. When a country's GDP rises over a consistent period of time, such an economy is said to be experiencing an expansion. On the other hand, a country's GDP reduces for a consistent period of time when the country is said to be on the recession.

GDP information tells you when to invest, what to invest in and how to structure your investments. This information can prove useful especially where you have a long term approach to investing. Even if you're a short term trader, it would be rewarding to know the kind of economic conditions you're dealing with and adjust your risk accordingly.

Inflation Data

Inflation refers to the consistent rise in the price of good and services in a particular economy. Inflation is usually measured using The Consumer Price Index (CPI) or the Producer Price Index (PPI). These two modes try to track the changes in the prices of goods and services and measures those changes in relation to other economic factors.

Inflation is important because it doesn't stand alone. Changes in inflation could be telling signs of impending danger. Other times, rising prices could signify good news. It could also be the resulting consequence of other things happening in the economy.

Unemployment Data

Unemployment is basically the percentage of people who are willing, able and are looking for jobs in an economy but cannot find those job. Thus, unemployment measures the rate at which the intellectual and physical talent of a country is being used. This data is usually related to the GDP for obvious reasons. A growing economy would employ more and vice versa.

This unemployment data should always be considered in line with the GDP. When the numbers don't add up then you should be careful about the moves you make until you're sure about why the numbers don't add up.

Putting it all together

While all the above mentioned are effective individually, a good investor trains himself to put the numbers together. Doing this ensures that you aren't making the wrong deduction from the information you have.

Also, the above-mentioned types of information are probably the most important but aren't the only relevant information to consider. Some others such as national debt, the balance of trade, a budget surplus, and deficit, etc. might prove instrumental in arriving at the best stock picks.

The Narrow View

This view concerns the individual companies you attempt to invest in. So let's say you think the United States economy is ripe for the taking. The economy is booming and the figures add up. Now you are looking to invest in particular companies within the US. How do you choose the best companies from the ones available? Having the right information is instrumental here as well.

Think about it. Why should the price of the stock of a company go up and down? To answer this question, you must take an elevated approach. Let's start with the position that people would pay a price they think the shares are worth. So if people think a company is worth more, then they'll be willing to pay more for the stock.

Next, we must consider what improves the prospect of a company. Why would people think the shares of a company would be worth more or less? They are usually looking at indications that lead to one of two conclusion – profit or loss. When people think a company would make money in the future, they would be willing to pay more for that company and the reverse is the truth as well.

What have just been said is the reason why paying attention to news about shares is important. Whether positive or negative, any form of news that gives an indication into the potential future earnings of a company would be considered good news and that would reflect in the price of the shares. This already gives you a framework for analyzing financial news. Thus you need to understand what the new information means to the potential future earnings of the company and factor that into your investment plans.

Now to the important question – what is the kind of information we are referring to in this case. The answer is simple. Anything and everything that fulfills the criteria mentioned above is important news to consider. However, we would discuss a few important ones below.

Economic Outlook

Top managers of listed companies usually release information about how they perceive their immediate future would be financial. This information is usually released annually, bi-annually or quarterly depending on the company and industry. The purpose of this information is to give an indication of what the company intends to do in the nearest future. Proper analysis of this kind of news can affect the way people buy and sell stocks which invariably increases the price of the stock.

Quarterly Earnings Report

This information as the name suggests is released once in 3 months. Basically, it is the income statement of a company for a period of 3 months. Economist considers financial information in circles. Thus, information released after a 3 month period about the earnings of a company is seen as a fair data about the financial health of such a company.

Quarterly earnings are also considered in relation to previous earnings data. Hence, if a company releases figures that show less earning, that is definitely saying something about the company's future.

Comments from CEOs

This might not seem like a big deal but when you consider the role a CEO plays in a company, you would realize it isn't so farfetched. The CEO of a company makes important decisions in a company. These decisions can affect the product or service of a company. For instance, if Elon Musk suddenly says he is beginning to lose patience with the antics of one of Tesla's spare part manufacturer, a lot of interpretation might be imputed into such a statement.

It could mean that Tesla would start the manufacture of that spare part. It could also mean production could be delayed in the future. Thus, when such a statement is considered alongside other statements then it could lead to a calculated deduction.

News on Merger and Acquisition

A merger is a situation whereby two companies come together to form a bigger company. Many times, companies merge to increase efficiency. For instance, where a timber company merges with a furniture maker, it could lead to reduced cost for the new company which leads to more profit for the shareholder. This is one of the many reasons why news on two companies merging would be considered a goldmine.

In fact, companies keep this sort of information close to the chest because it could make the price of the stock rise rapidly. This makes the merger more expensive.

Acquisition is the situation whereby a company purchases the shares of another company up to a threshold where that company has control over the acquired company. An acquisition has a similar effect as a merger since two companies are coming together to become one as well. Though as earlier stated, this kind of news usually gets to the press lately. A smart investor might, however, figure it out before it hits the press.

Timing Matters

All the information we just discussed cannot be put to good use if you ignore the element of timing. Financial information has a cycle of relevance. After a particular time, the information gets priced into the stock. At that point, it's already too late to use that information.

For instance, let's assume that Google is about to release its new quarterly earnings. If you are a long term investor who likes to hold stocks for years, this information might not mean much to you. However, if you profit from daily spikes and dips in the market, you should probably be on a lookout for the news.

Expected News Vs Actual News

These two concepts can be executed as a strategy in itself. It is important to understand the distinction between the two and how to use it to your advantage. No matter how properly guided the secrets of a company are, there are always people in the know. Before news hits the press, an analyst always has a fair idea of what the new figures would hold.

This is not so farfetched as the activities of a company in the market can be measured. Also, investors are usually armed with price states. These stats can lead to a reasonable prediction of what future data would look like.

So it is not uncommon to find projections about incoming news before the news gets to the public. The resultant effect of this is that market participants start to act as if the information has been released already. If the projections favor a buy, people immediately start buying as if the news is already out. When the news is finally released, the price of the shares doesn't respond since the response happened days or weeks ago.

However, the price doesn't respond only when the actual news matches the projections. When the information is against the projection, it could lead to a rapid change in price. An example is where people think the sales of a company would increase and they already priced in that supposition but real data shows stagnant or dropping sales. This immediately changes people's opinion about the stock and invariably it leads to a dip in the price.

How does all of this affect you as a newbie? That's simple. You always have to be conscious of this fact and be wary of making decisions when there is a possibility of an upset.

Where to Get Credible News

As we have noted earlier, there are various news sources scattered over the Internet. Most of which can be confusing when you don't know what to look for. However, there are certain news websites and mediums that ensure credibility and simplicity. This part discusses a few of those sources and what you can get for them.

Bloomberg

Bloomberg is a mainstream financial news platform owned by Michael Bloomberg. The media hasn't provided financial news through their website and their electronic media platforms. Aside from regular news, you'll also find analysis and study of several industries and particular companies. This platform is unique for presenting financial information in a language that isn't too difficult to understand for a newbie.

Additionally, they offer live feeds on several asset classes including stocks, bonds, currencies, commodities, and derivatives.

Reuters

Just like Bloomberg, Reuters offers investors in-depth market analysis just as the news drops. The platform offers this product through a variety of mediums including print and social media. You can also subscribe to the newsletter to get regular market updates from your mail.

Google Alerts

You might be wondering how Google alert would be a good source of financial news. Well, we are about to tell you why. Imagine you just purchased Google stocks, wouldn't you like to know when any news related to Google breaks on the Internet? That's where Google alert comes in. You could use this service rendered by Google to track news related to anything you have invested in. Thus, you can be sure never to miss out on valuable news as soon as it breaks.

Chapter 10: Value Investing

The interesting thing about his investing style is he really doesn't pay attention to what the current price of the company is. Instead, he looks at long term value. It may well turn out that the stock of a company seems fairly high by today's standards. However, to Buffett, the stock is actually cheap in light of its future value.

The secret to value investing is future value. You basically would have to look at the track record of the company, its current operations, and health, as well as the health of the industry it's in. You then project this information in the future factoring in potential future conditions. Once you have a fairly clear picture, you then buy in, and it's important to note that you basically don't leave. That's the whole point of value investing.

You buy and you hold. You're playing the long game. This strategy is strictly for people who buy long. Now, fresh from our discussion about position trading, you might be asking yourself, well if I buy long then I might be suffering opportunity cost because I could have been making more money in the short term buying a more volatile stock?

Believe me, if you play the biotech or internet stocks, they can be quite volatile. It's not uncommon for traders to make thousands of dollars every single day of the volatility of these stocks. They move that quickly. Warren Buffett doesn't care about any of that. Instead, his game is to basically hold the company for several years or even decades and at the end of that long period, the stock has split many times or has gone up in value so much.

If you ever need proof of this, look at his main investment vehicle, Berkshire Hathaway. Can you imagine if you have bought Berkshire Hathaway in the 80s? You would be a millionaire many times over today. That's how awesome of an investor Warren Buffet is. He's all about the long game. He's all about patient investing.

Now, value investing may not fit your investment goals. If your immediate goal is to have your money appreciate by 10% or 15% per year, value investing may not be a slam dunk. You have to understand that value investing looks at growth over time. It may be substantial growth. We're talking about the may be company's stock price doubling or even tripling, but it's anybody's guess when this will exactly happen.

It's not uncommon for a stock to only appreciate 5% the next year, and then the year after that goes up to 20%, and then dips down to 10%, so on and so forth. But when you average everything out, it turns out that the stock has actually doubled, tripled, or even quadrupled in price.

How to do Value Investing

Warren Buffett is known for simply reading the financial statements of a company, as well as their financial papers in the comfort of his office. He would then make phone calls to make million-dollar stock purchases. That's all he does. He usually never goes to the actual company. He usually never reads the paper or checks out the news regarding the company.

All he pays attention to are their numbers. I don't expect you to master the game so well that you only need to see numbers. This is why you need to pay attention to the following factors.

Focus on CASH FLOW

Solid companies have cash flow volumes that justify their price. The company must be generating revenue. Even if it is no earning a profit, it must have enough cash flow to justify its price either now or some point in the future. Depending on how speculative the stock is, cash flow is determined by either P/E or price-to-book.

(P/E) Price to Earnings Ratio: The company's earnings per share is cross referenced to its current stock price. For example: if a company is earning $1 per share is trading at $20 per share, its P/E ratio is 20. This is an indication of cash flow value in reference to its current price. If you're going to use P/E as your cash flow factor, you should compare different stocks that have the same fundamentals (industry positioning, book value, growth factors, and others).

Price to book Ratio: After reading a company's balance sheet, you will be aware of all the assets a company has. After proper depreciation and discounting, whatever amount left is the liquidation value of the company's assets. In other words, if you were going to liquidate the company and get cash for all assets and you take out whatever debt the company owes, what's left is its book value. Price to book is the ratio of how many times the company's book value is multiplied to produce its current per share value. For example: if you have a company that has a book value of $10 per share and it trades for $100 per share, it's price to book value is 10.

Please note that there are many other cash flow-based value calculation methods but P/E and price to book are the most common and are enough to guide any beginner investor. As you become more proficient at trading, you might want to scale up using other methods at calculating cash flow.

Focus on Industry Leaders

The first thing you need to do is to look for industry leaders or potential leaders in an industry. It's important to look at solid companies. These companies are doing something right. They're making money. They have made an impact. They've got their act together. It's important to focus on these qualities.

The problem with a lot of stock out there is that a lot of them are sold based on hype and potential. For example, Twitter traded as high as the low 40s because people are optimistic that somehow, someway, it's going to make money. Its valuation wasn't really based on how the company was run, how much money it was making, its position in the industry. None of that matter. All the focus was on potential growth.

Not so with value investing. You look at the actual position of the company and the fact that it is already making money. You start with that fact. The company has to be already well positioned. This doesn't mean that the company has already dominated its industry nor is the number one player. It can be an up and comer. What's important is that it has its house in order.

It must have Solid Financials

A key indicator that a company has its financial house in order is that it has zero to low debt. A company that has almost no debt and a low stock price is actually quite underpriced. This is the kind of combination that Warren Buffett gets excited about. He knows that chances are quite good that for some reason or other, the market simply is not acknowledging the solid fundamentals of a company. And one key factor in that is its debt exposure.

If the company has almost zero debt and a low stock price and a solid market or industry presence, then the company has a good chance of being a good value investment. However, you need to look at other factors as well.

The Company is in a Growing Industry

Now, can you imagine doing your research in stocks and finding a company that is a soon to be the industry leader, or is already an industry leader and has zero debt? It is also very profitable currently. On top of all of this, its stock is fairly low as measured by price per earnings ratio (P/E). Sounds like a slam dunk, right?

Well, hold your horses. Pay attention to the company that industry is in. It may well turn out that that company is the only gem in that industry because that industry is basically going downhill. In that situation, that company is probably going to have a bleak future. Its stock price might look good now, but it's only a matter of time until that company implodes or has to reinvent itself and enter another industry.

Pay attention to the industry. Is it under a tremendous amount of disruption? Or is it still a growing industry? The problem with industries that are under a tremendous amount of disruption is that you really don't know the direction the industry would go.

For example, the Eastman Kodak Corporation was the top dog of the photographic materials industry. Thanks to the rise of digital cameras, the photographic material industry is a shadow of its former self. It still exists in a very limited form, but it's definitely not big enough to sustain a company that's as gigantic as the Eastman Kodak.

Do you see how this works? And the problem was that the industry that was under serious disruption during the 90s and early 2000s. Steer clear from companies that are under disruption because it's anybody's guess what the ultimate direction of the technology or business strategies of the companies in that industry.

Heavy Cash Flow and large Cash Position

Another factor value investors look at is how much cash a company has in its book. Now, this is the key indicator of how well that company is run. If a company is profitable but it essentially just burns up its remaining cash on research and development, the company might not be a solid value investment because it's essentially spending a lot of money to make a lot of money.

Ultimately, it's basically just trying to tread water. This is not always the case. It also depends on the industry. Still, if you notice that a company has a lot of cash on its balance sheet and almost zero debt, that company is doing something right and if you can see that the cash at hand is growing over time, then this is a key indicator that this company may be a solid value investment, with everything else being equal.

Pay attention to accounts receivable. While a healthy level of accounts receivables is fine, a company that has an extremely high A/R level merits further and deeper analysis. It might be having a tough time collecting and you need to be very careful about how they log these. The company might only seem like it is worth a lot of money.

"Underappreciated Stocks"

Warren Buffett makes a big deal about underappreciated stocks. In fact, in many of his interviews, he talks about buying stocks that are under appreciated. Now, a lot of people would define "underappreciated stocks" as companies whose stock prices are a bargain compared to other companies in the Dow Jones Industrial Average.

This is a misconception. A stock is underappreciated in classical value investment terms not based on how it compares to other companies but based on its potential future value. So, in that context, a company that is selling for $50 a share now while other companies in its industry are selling for $40 a share, and its rate of appreciation is somewhat the same or slightly higher than the Dow Jones Industrial Average, can still be an underappreciated stock.

I know it sounds shocking, why? Compared to how it can grow in the future and what its potential fully realized value is in the long-term future, its current stock price may be a bargain. Always keeps this in mind when doing value investing. Value investing doesn't necessarily mean penny pincher. It doesn't necessarily mean looking for discount stocks. It can very well mean that and you're basically buying at an immediate bargain compared to other stocks, but you should also factor in future value.

The stock may seem like it's well appreciated now, but given all the factors that I've outlined above, it might still be underappreciated and you would do well to lock in now. Remember, your strategy is to buy and hold. You're not looking to buy on a dip and unload on a recovery. You're just buying and holding for long term value.

The Risks of Value Investing

As solid as value investing may be, especially if you are setting money aside for your retirement, it also has its risks. First of all, let me point out the obvious. This investing strategy requires a very long-time horizon. In fact, you shouldn't care about whether the stock spikes up or sinks down. All you care about is where the stock would be five, ten, fifteen, thirty years from now.

This is the time horizon value investor's focus on. They look at the overall value of their portfolio and they focus on how much farther they would be ahead in dollars and cents when they cash out several years from now. This may seem good on paper, but it's not uncommon for a stock that you thought has a solid value to go through some rough years.

This happens quite a bit. When you buy the stock, it may be trading at $40 per share and then the next year, it goes through a rough patch and it sinks to $30. Then the year after that, it sinks another $10, to $20. At that point, you may be thinking to yourself that you made the wrong call but assuming that you did your homework properly, you really have nothing to worry about because you're in for the long game.

You're not holding the stock for just three years, you're holding the stock basically as an heirloom because you're going to cash out ten, twenty or thirty years from now. By that point, the stock price may have doubled or even tripled. Do you see how this works? Don't let the long-time horizons get you down and scare you if the company goes through some reversals.

Another risk for value investing involves opportunity costs. If you have adopted a swing trading strategy, you may have been better off because you could have ridden several stocks up and down and realized faster gains. However, the whole opportunity cost argument is really only valuable if you're in a hurry. If on the other hand, you are playing a long investment game with a long timeframe, then the opportunity costs are not really that big of an issue.

There's still an issue because you could have probably bought a better value stock, but all in all, the whole idea of wishing that you bought something else that you could have traded rapidly isn't an issue at all for a value investor.

Chapter 11: Easy Ways to Reduce Risks When Investing in the Stock Market

Working with the stock market can be a great way to help you earn some money. There may be a lot of different types of investments that you can choose from, but none is going to give you as many options as you can get from investing in the stock market. You can choose from many different types of companies to invest in, you can choose the amount of risks that you want to take, and even which industries you would like to pick from.

With all these benefits, you may wonder why everyone hasn't entered into the stock market to make their money as well. The truth is, there is a certain risk that comes with being in this kind of market. And as a beginner who hasn't had much time to research and learn more about the market, these risks can seem overwhelming.

No one goes into the stock market with the idea that they are going to lose a lot of money. They get in hoping that they can make a steady profit and, over time, even replace their full-time income to see some great results. But in order to do this, it is important to learn how to manage all of your risks with this investment. This chapter is going to explore some of the things that you can do, such as putting in some stop-loss points, sticking with a strategy, and more, to help you reduce your risks and get the most out of this investment.

Avoid the Crowd Mentality

There are a lot of people who rely on their neighbors, friends, and other people in their lives in order to make some important decisions about their stock picks. But you need to realize that most of these people either know nothing about the stock market or they want you to react in a certain manner because it will help their own stocks make money. When you go with the crowd mentality and start taking advice from lots of different people, you will also find that there is an issue with not being able to think about things clearly.

As an investor in the stock market, you need to make sure that you are not following along with the decisions of other people. You should always be afraid when others are acting greedy for a stock, but then act greedy when others are being afraid of that stock. This will serve you much better because, often, when lots of people go after one stock, it ends up backfiring on them all because prices get too high while dividends are low.

Pick Your Strategy and Don't Change It

There are a lot of great strategies that we have talked about in this guidebook. Many of them are going to provide you with some level of success. In fact, some of the most successful traders already use a lot of these strategies to help them earn money. The problem in most cases is not that the strategies don't work. It is more an issue of the beginner trader who is either not understanding how the strategy works, or picks a strategy and then switch away from it right in the middle of the trade.

If you end up switching your strategy through the trade, you are going to run into trouble. You went into the trade with one strategy and switching it up will ensure that you fail. Yes, there are times when a strategy won't work as well as you want, but you will suffer fewer losses if you stick with the plan and finish out the trade. When the trade is done, you can easily go back and try out a different strategy if you didn't care for the first one.

Make Sure the Emotions Don't Come into Play

When the emotions come out to play, that is the end of your trade. You will stop thinking rationally and will start taking too many risks in the hopes of earning money. This is never a good idea. If you notice that your emotions are starting to influence the decisions you make, rather than the charts determining your decisions, then it is time to take a step back and even take a break to help limit your losses.

This is why it is so important to come up with a good trading plan right from the beginning. This plan is going to list out your strategy, which stocks you are going to invest in, the amount of money and time that you will invest in that stock, and even the conditions when you will enter and exit the trade to get the most out of it. Without this plan, your emotions can easily get in the way. But when you make a plan and keep on it, you are going to see that it is easier to make rational decisions that can limit your losses and increase your profits.

Only Invest What You Can Afford

While some brokers will offer you to trade on the margin, which means that you can borrow money for a trade, that is not a good idea. You should pick an amount that you are comfortable with losing, and then never invest more than that. It can be frustrating to give up some good trades because you don't have enough money to take them on.

Investing the amount you can afford can help out with the risk. No one wants to lose money on the market, but it happens when you are a beginner. If you stick with an amount that you are comfortable with losing, it won't be as big of a deal because it was already money that you put aside.

If you trade on the margin or spend more money than you can afford, then it is going to end up badly. When the trade is done, you may owe money back and will have to figure out a way to pay all of that back as well. This can be hard on a beginner, but it is much better than increasing your risks and losing out on everything because you made the wrong prediction. As time goes on and you spend more time in the market learning the ropes and understanding how it all works, you can start to do some of those bigger trades.

Never Try to Time the Market

Some beginners will try to time when they get into the market exactly. They want to purchase at the exact low and the exact high that price of the stock hits. While this would guarantee that you are going to pay the least and make the most on your investment, it is really hard to time the market this way. And trying to do so is going to add to your risk and makes it hard to actually do well with making a profit.

The problem with this is that the market moves really fast. Being able to time out the market may seem like a great option, but it is much easier to miss these amounts if you try to wait them out. Instead of waiting for those exact times to occur, it is better to just watch the market, set up your stop-loss points, and get out once they are hit.

Yes, this means that at times, you are going to miss out on some of the profits. The stock price may continue to go up and you won't be able to earn all of the potential profit. But what this does is to ensure that you get to walk out of the trade with some profit. If you stick with the stock too long, and you don't put those stops into place, you may stay in too long and not be able to get any profits or even lose money. These stop points can be much better to ensure that you will be able to actually earn a profit and can protect you from any unexpected downturns in the market.

Always Have Realistic Expectations for Your Trades

It is easy to get caught up in the idea that you can make a lot of money. You hear about other people who got started with the stock market and were able to make it rich. The fact is, many of these people had to work in the market for a very long time before they saw results. Very few investors are able to get rich overnight with the stock market.

While you can make some money on the stock market, you need to be careful with how high your expectations go. You are not going to make it rich on one trade, and you will probably need to spend a few years or more in the stock market before you can see more than a little bit of profit from the trades that you make.

This is not meant to discourage you. It is simply to help you understand more about how the market works and to set you up better for success. It is important to have some realistic expectations when you get started. When you do this, it is much easier for you to make smart decisions, to plan things out better, and more. This way, you can actually make a profit, rather than chasing after schemes that promise a lot of money but won't earn you anything in the process.

There is going to be a little bit of risk that comes with investing in the stock market. Any time that you invest your money anywhere, you will find that there will be some risks involved. But if you follow the steps above, you will be able to reduce your risk as much as possible.

Conclusion

Let me hope it was informative and has provided you with all the tools that you need to get started on swing trading. I also hope that the tools will help you reach your goals regardless of what they may be. Just because you have finished reading the book it does not mean there is nothing else left to learn in swing trading, the only way to find the mastery skill you seek is by expanding your horizons.

The next step is to do whatever is needed in order to ensure that you succeed. With swing trading, you cannot stop reading and gathering new information every day; therefore, keep the book close for reference and check out other education sources. You will find that you still need help choosing new trades, styles, strategies, indicators among others even after getting experience. As such, you will most likely have better results by keeping records and journals on what you learned.

Studies show that consistency helps to break down complex tasks such as swing trading. Therefore, you can only meet your targets by having clear plans and schedules. Even if it seems hard, set your own goals and pursue them; in the end, you will be glad you did. Keep in mind the risk management plans; they take care of your account. Do a lot of practice with demo accounts before venturing into the real trading world.

Since you have completed your initial preparation, it is important to understand that it is just a preparation, a part of the bigger picture. Your highest chance of overall success will come from taking the time to analyze and learn as many essential skills as possible. Only by using the preparedness as a springboard to greater achievements will a swing trader be able to trade well, knowing that they have prepared for anything and everything that the market throws at them.

Finally, if you found the book useful, in any way, please leave a review it will be highly appreciated.

Don't miss out!

Visit the website below and you can sign up to receive emails whenever Leonardo Turner publishes a new book. There's no charge and no obligation.

https://books2read.com/r/B-A-XCJI-HEPZ

BOOKS 2 READ

Connecting independent readers to independent writers.

Did you love *Stock Market Investing For Beginners Learn Strategies To Profit In Stock Trading, Day Trading And Generate Passive Income*? Then you should read *Real Estate Investing Blueprint For Beginners How To Create Passive Income On Properties To Escape The Rat Race And Reach Financial freedom* by Leonardo Turner!

This guidebook is going to take some time to explain all of the things that you need to know to get started with your first rental property. We will discuss the importance of financial freedom and how real estate investing, especially with rental properties, will be able to help you to reach those goals of financial freedom.

From there, we are going to dive right into the process of searching for and finding the perfect rental properties for your needs. We will look at how you can look for a property, how to get the right financing, the importance of doing an analysis on the property, and even how to determine your return on investment to determine if you are actually going to be able to earn an income on all of the work that you do.

In the final section, we are going to discuss what you will need to do when you actually own the property. We will look at how to find the right tenants, how to maintain and fix up the home, how to collect rental payments, and even how you may work with a property manager to help you get the income, without having to be there and help your tenants all of the time.

Getting started in rental properties is going to take some time, dedication, and so much more. But for those who are looking for a good way to increase their financial freedom, and who want to be able to own their own time, then this is one of the best investment opportunities for you to go with. When you are ready to get started with your own rental property investment, make sure to check out this guidebook to help you out!

9 781393 360346